MW00885045

WATER BATH CANNING AND PRESERVING COOKBOOK FOR BEGINNERS

SERENA FOSTER

© Copyright 2023 by Serena Foster All rights reserved.
Water Bath Canning and Preserving Cookbook for Beginners

ISBN: 979-8374663976
10 9 8 7 6 5 4 3 2 1

All Rights reserved

GET YOUR BONUS NOW!

Greetings and welcome! It's an honor to be speaking to the best audience in the world. Thank you for purchasing my book "Water Bath Canning and Preserving Cookbook for Beginners". I'm hoping that this book will help you get ready for any upcoming disasters.

I would want to give you a copy of "Freeze Drying Cookbook For Preppers," a joint effort with Mark Rivers that offers novel preservation techniques, as a gesture of my appreciation.

Thank you again for your support, and I hope both publications will be helpful resources for you.

To Download your bonus, scan the QR code below!

The bonus is **100% free,** with no strings attached.
You don't need to enter any personal details.

Table of Contents

Introduction

The history of food canning and preservation is quite long. The practice of canning food dates back to the early 1800s and was originally used to preserve food for long trips or during times of famine. Indeed, canning is a very versatile process that can be used to preserve a variety of foods.

Canning is considered one of the most recent and widely used methods for the protection of food items. Without a doubt, canning the food item keeps them fresh and maintains their taste to be served to people through different seasons in a year. Nowadays, people can and preserve for various reasons. Even with all the industrial preserving approaches at their all-time best, most of us like the idea of canning and preserving our own foods in the comfort of our homes.

You may discover instructions for water bath canning and food preservation of various kinds in this cookbook. You can cook and preserve something whether you are a novice or an expert canner. From jams, jellies, pickles, salsa, and sauces to vegetables, fruits, and meats, there is something for everyone in this cookbook.

At the end of this cookbook, we've also included two bonus chapters for food ideas you can prepare without an appliance and food ideas you can prepare while you're away from home. So, if you're looking for something new and fun, and are stuck for ideas, then this book is a must-read.

Chapter 1.   Canning & Preserving 101

If you tell someone that canning is a complicated and unsafe practice of home-food preservation, you are wrong. You only need to determine the type of method that can be used to preserve foods according to the pH level of the food. The main goal of canning foods is to remove oxygen molecules, reduce or stop the enzymatic activity, and inhibit or kill the microorganisms such as bacteria, yeast, and molds. Because the multiplication time is fast and ranges between 10-30 mins. But canned foods tend to retain their quality and taste better as compared to frozen foods.

For many decades, salting, drying, brining, and soaking foods in honey are the old traditional techniques used to keep the foods safe for consumption even after months. The food canning and preservation techniques in the guide are a combination of old traditional techniques and practices and new scientific justifications to offer food to people that is safe and delicious to enjoy even after a couple of weeks and months. These methods include fermentation, pressure canning, and water bath canning.

Despite the widespread use of different canning methods, the United States Department of Agriculture only recognizes two canning processes: water bath canning and pressure canning.

Water Bath Canning

One of the simplest methods as a preservation practice is water bath canning. This practice is widely used for foods that are highly acidic in nature, pickles, fruits. It works by creating an anaerobic environment in a vacuum-sealed jar. The reduction of enzyme activity and the suppression of microbial growth are the goals of producing an acidic environment.

In this method, a jar filled with food is placed in boiling water, but the jar's lid is loosely sealed. The heat of the boiling water increases the food temperature to 100°C or 212°F. Due to heat, the food starts to expand, and air inside the jar travels out, making the jar air-free. After the food is processed, the jar is removed from the water bath and allowed to cool. A vacuum seal is formed with the contraction of food, which is confirmed by a sound created by canning lids. Vacuum sealed jars to keep the food contamination-free but inhibit microorganisms' entrance or growth inside the jar.

Pressure Canning

For the safe preservation of low-acidic foods, pressure canning is the most proper method. This includes seafood, meat, non-pickled vegetables, and a combination of high and low acidic foods like meat sauces, stew, and soups. Considering the pH of such foods is more than 4.6, the temperature for processing is 116°C. Low acidic foods require high temperatures for processing to destroy the microorganisms, their spores, and the toxins produced in the food. High temperature is created in pressure canners which are specialized to develop a pressurized environment.

When the water starts to boil, it releases steam via a steam vent pipe. It is then capped with the weighted gauge to create pressure and increase the temperature up to 116°C. A combined effect of time and pressure have given to food inside the pressure canners kills all the spoilers present in the food to create a shelf-stable, safe, and preserved canned food. Water bath canning and pressure canning are identical processes with only a temperature and method modification.

Fermenting

Fermentation or Lacto-fermentation are the two common names used for fermenting fruits and vegetables. It is a process that is a source of attraction for good microorganisms found in nature. Good or beneficial microorganisms are probiotics, which can transform sugars in food items into lactic acid. The conversion of sugars into lactic acid results in creating delicious, fermented foods. This helps in protecting the food items safe from food spoilers or toxins produced by harmful microorganisms.

Commonly used methods for fermenting include brining, dry salting, the sauerkraut method, and kimchi style.

The common function of all these methods is that they remove moisture from fruits, vegetables, and other foods to create a brine. Brining is important to allow foods to undergo a safe fermentation process. Because good bacteria are produced during brining and promote the production of acid for safe fermentation of foods. During fermentation, it is crucial to keep the food beneath the brine, or else molds and yeast will grow, and food will not remain safe for consumption.

Because everyone has different taste preferences, the duration of fermentation varies from short to long ferments until a pungent smell is produced in the food. Smell the food, and if you find the right smell, you can seal the jars to be stored in refrigerators because the fermentation process slows down at low temperatures.

Chapter 2.   A Brief History of Water Bath Canning

The water bath canning process has a rich history that dates back centuries. It's a method that has helped generations preserve fresh farm produce and enjoy seasonal fruits and vegetables all year-round. Let us take a journey through the evolution of this time-tested food preservation technique.

The Beginnings of Canning

The water bath canning process has its roots in the late 18th century when French scientist Nicolas Appert discovered the art of preserving food through heating and sealing it in airtight containers. Appert's pioneering work laid the foundation for modern canning methods, including water bath canning.

Appert initially used champagne bottles sealed with cork and sealing wax for his preservation process, but as the need arose, he later transitioned to using glass jars. His innovation led to an increased adoption of the canning process due to its effectiveness in preserving food without affecting its taste, texture, or nutritional value.

The art of home canning was introduced to America during the 19th century by settlers who brought with them their European traditions. As farming communities began to develop across America, preserving and storing surplus produce to prepare for long winters became crucial to families' survival. Water bath canning emerged as an affordable and practical solution for home gardeners.

Development of Water Bath Canners

With the increasing popularity of home canning throughout the late 19th and early 20th centuries, several metalworking companies started developing specialized equipment for water bath canning. By the 1920s, home canning had become a flourishing industry, with numerous canners available in various sizes and designs.

The importance of water bath canning surged during World War II, when food rationing became common practice in many countries. In America, the government encouraged home-front gardening through the "Victory Gardens" movement to grow and preserve food at home. As a result, a new wave of interest in preserving fruits and vegetables emerged.

Modern Innovations and Techniques

Over the years, both equipment used in water bath canning and the process itself have evolved to offer better safety, efficiency, and convenience. Today, we have automated water bath canners that control temperature precisely and use a timer to ensure the process is completed accurately.

The impact of technological innovations has also been felt in the realm of food preservation science. Modern research focuses on ensuring that water bath canning recipes are safe and healthy, minimizing botulism risk while maintaining flavor and nutrition.

The history of water bath canning is an intriguing story of creativity, practicality, and adaptability – both in preserving nature's bounty and withstanding the test of time. As we revel in our modern kitchens with state-of-the-art equipment, let us not forget that our ancestors are responsible for this practical method of food preservation that plays such an integral part in our culinary heritage.

Chapter 3.   Must-Have Tools & Equipment

As with any trip, embarking on the journey of home canning requires some specific gear. You won't need a new sleeping bag or a tent, but just like those tools, the canning equipment you purchase will be used over and over—for years, if not decades. So, although a little up-front investment is required, it will provide returns for years.

Others may quibble with our recommendations, but if you have a good selection of cooking implements, many of them can be used for more specific canning tools.

Water Bath Canner: Water bath canners are huge stockpots with adequate depth to submerge the jars and a height to accommodate the canning process. Larger 21-quart canners hold 7-quart jars or 9-pint jars. This is the right size for you if you plan to make large batches of pickles or canned tomatoes. Smaller 12-quart canners hold 4-quart jars or 7-pint jars, which is the perfect size for processing small-batch jams or sauces. Do be aware that some water bath canners are not appropriate for certain types of stoves—for instance, induction or glass-top stoves. Check your range owner's manual before choosing a specific canner.

Any large stockpot can be used for canning, but it might be difficult to find a suitable size, as most are tall and narrow or short and wide, neither of which will do the trick.

Canning Rack: A rack is required to maintain the jars above the water level in the cooking vessel. Most canners come with an aluminum rack. These work great but will rust over time. If you are planning to do a lot of water bath canning, splurge on a stainless-steel rack.

If you use a stockpot as a water bath canner, you will have to purchase a separate canning rack. Canning racks of all sizes can be found online.

Large Pot: Because most foods need to be cooked before canning, you definitely need a large pot. A 5-quart pot is large enough to prepare small batches of jams, pickles, sauces, and so on. To be safe, though, you should get a pot or Dutch oven that holds at least 8 quarts. The larger pot reduces the chances of jam or pickles boiling over—and of you getting hit with hot, splattering jam. Plus, a larger pot ensures that all the ingredients are heated through, thus helping make your home-canned product safe. Avoid aluminum or cast iron; instead choose enamel, ceramic, or stainless steel. Products containing aluminum or cast iron will have an unpleasant metallic taste if they contain acidic components.

Canning Jars: It is absolutely imperative to have approved canning jars with two-piece lids. Although Mom may have used empty mayonnaise or pickle jars, please refrain from following this tradition. Jars used in commercial canning these days are designed for a single use only and not the home canning process. The glass is not as heavy nor as sturdy as that of approved canning jars. It's simply not worth the risk of shattered jars and injuries from glass shards.

Lids And Rings: New boxes of approved canning jars come complete with two-piece metal lids, which include a sealable lid and the ring that keeps it in place on the jar. You can also purchase additional rings and lids separately. Most sealable lids are designed for one use only, so do not try to reuse them. Rings can be used over and over, but because they are metal, they may become rusted or bent, at which point they must be discarded. Reusable plastic lids are fairly new to the market; they require a slightly different sealing technique, so be sure to follow the individual brand directions.

Towels: We recommend placing tea towels or terrycloth dish towels on the counter to cushion the jars when setting them down. Towels help keep jars from slipping while they are being filled and insulate hot jars after processing. A clean towel, dipped in water or white vinegar, should be used to wipe down jar lips after filling but before adding the two-piece lids. Vinegar is especially helpful when you are canning items that may be greasy; otherwise, a towel moistened with water works fine.

Jar Lifter: A jar lifter grabs the hot jars and helps you lift them from the water bath canner. It is a handy implement and the most effective way to remove hot jars without burning your fingers.

Food Scale: Some people consider a food scale a necessity. However, most of the recipes in this book include ingredient amounts in cups or by number of items, as well as by weight. A food scale might come in handy when you aren't quite sure about how large to chop the fruit or whether you have enough product on hand to make the recipe. Check ingredient weights with a food scale in these situations.

Funnel: A wide-mouth jar funnel is my favorite canning implement. While you can fill jars without a funnel, using one makes the job easier and less messy. Look for a funnel that is specially designed to fit both regular and wide-mouth canning jars.

Bubble Remover: This implement is designed to remove bubbles from filled jars and is most often used when canning fruits or pickles. Any long, nonmetallic device, like a chopstick, can be used instead, but the bubble remover is thin and thus easier to use and more effective.

Magnetic Lid Grabber: Although it is no longer necessary to sterilize jar lids before use, the lids do need to be clean, so many of us still preheat them in simmering water. This tool lets you grab the lid and lift it out of the water, saving you from scalded fingers. You can use tongs to pick up the lids, but this tool works like magic.

Headspace Measuring Tool: Every canning recipe requires a specific bit of headspace, an empty area between the top of the container and the lid. This angled tool measures just how much headspace you have so you can adjust the product amount if necessary. The screw rings on the jars usually do this as well, with the bottom ring indicating ½-inch headspace and the top ring indicating ¼-inch headspace. Or you can always use a ruler.

Digital Thermometer: A candy or deep-fry thermometer can help ensure that you have reached the gelling point if you frequently prepare jam and fruit preserves. 8 degrees above the boiling point is the gelling point. Other ways to check for jam gelling, like the plate method or the spoon method (described here), are less precise but can be used in a pinch. A thermometer assures that your jams are perfectly set, neither too syrupy nor too thick.

Cheesecloth Or Jelly Bag: Using fine-weave cheesecloth or a jelly bag is the easiest way to strain fruit for jelly. Cheesecloth also comes in handy when using whole spices in pickling or when infusing syrups and vinegars.

Chapter 4.   How to Sanitized & Prepare Canning Jars

One of the most crucial steps in water bath canning is properly sanitizing and preparing your jars to ensure the food's safety and flavor. This chapter will guide you through the process of sanitizing and preparing your jars for successful water bath canning.

1. Choose the right jars: The first step in sanitizing and preparing your canning jars is to make sure you have chosen the correct type of jar. Be sure to use high-quality glass canning jars specifically designed for home canning, such as Mason or Ball jars. These jars can easily withstand high temperatures without cracking or breaking during the canning process.

2. Inspect your jars carefully: Before you start the sanitization process, inspect each jar for any cracks, chips, or other defects that may prevent a proper seal from forming or cause breakage during the canning process. Discard any damaged jars and select only those in perfect condition for your water bath canning.

3. Wash your jars thoroughly: Wash all selected jars in warm soapy water before sanitizing them. Use a clean sponge or dishcloth and pay particular attention to the inside rims where lids will make contact with the jar edges. Rinse each jar well under clear running water to remove any soap residue.

4. Prepare the water bath for sanitizing: Fill a large pot with enough water to cover your jars completely, allowing 1-2 inches of extra headspace to accommodate boiling. Place a rack on the bottom of the pot to prevent direct contact between the jars and the bottom of the pot, which may cause breakage due to uneven heat distribution.

5. Heat the water bath: Bring the water in the bath pot to a rolling boil. While the water is heating, arrange your jars on a heat-resistant surface near the pot, such as a kitchen counter covered with a towel.

6. Submerge the jars in boiling water: Once the water reaches a rolling boil, carefully lower each jar into the water bath using jar lifters or tongs. Ensure the jars are fully submerged and that there is enough space between them for water to circulate freely.

7. Boil the jars for 10 mins: Allow the jars to boil for at least 10 mins to sanitize them completely, adjusting for altitude if necessary (add one min of boiling time for every 1,000 feet above sea level).

8. Prepare your lids and bands: While your jars are boiling, get your sealing lids and bands ready. Follow the manufacturer's instructions for pretreating your lids and bands (some may need to be simmered in hot water before use). Keep lids warm until you are ready to use them, but do not boil.

9. Remove and drain jars from boiling water: After sanitizing your jars in the boiling water, carefully remove them using jar lifters or tongs and place them upright on a clean, dry towel on your work surface. Let excess water drain from the jars before filling them with food.

10. Fill your jars with prepared food: Now that your jars are sanitized and prepared, you are ready to fill them with food following specific instructions based on recipes in this cookbook, ensuring proper headspace is maintained for successful canning.

By following these steps diligently, you will ensure that your canning process starts with perfectly sanitized and prepared canning jars necessary for safe, long-lasting preservation of your homegrown fruits and veggies!

Chapter 5.   Steps For Water Bath Canning

Water bath canning is a simple and effective way to preserve your favorite fruits, pickles, jams, and jellies. This method uses boiling water to heat the jars and create an airtight seal that prevents spoilage. In this chapter, we will walk you through the essential steps for successful water bath canning.

STEP 1. Gather Your Supplies

Before you begin, make sure you have all the necessary equipment:

Jars: Choose proper size Mason jars with two-piece canning lids.

Canner: A large pot with rack designed for water bath canning, or a regular large pot with a trivet or folded dish towel on the bottom.

Jar lifter: A handy tool to lift hot jars out of boiling water.

Funnel: This helps ensure a clean transfer of food into jars.

Bubble remover: Essential for removing air bubbles from jars.

Kitchen towels: Useful for wiping jar rims and protecting surfaces from hot jars.

STEP 2. Prepare Your Food

Wash and prepare your recipe ingredients according to your chosen recipe. Make sure you follow all the instructions for cutting, peeling, and cooking your produce.

STEP 3. Sterilize the Jars and Lids

To prevent contamination, sterilize the jars by either boiling them in a large pot of water for 10 mins or running them through the dishwasher on its hottest setting without detergent. Keep the jars hot until they are filled.

Bring the two-piece lids to a simmer in a separate small saucepan but don't boil them.

STEP 4. Pack Your Jars

Carefully fill each jar with prepared food, leaving enough headspace as recommended by your recipe (typically 1/4-inch to 1/2-inch). Use a funnel for neat filling and mitigation of spills.

STEP 5. Release Air Bubbles

Use a bubble remover or another non-metallic utensil to run down the sides of each jar to release trapped air bubbles. Then, add more food if necessary to maintain the correct headspace.

STEP 6. Clean and Seal the Jars

Use a damp paper towel or kitchen towel to wipe the rims of each jar clean. This step ensures proper sealing. Place the lids on top and secure them with rings, making sure not to overtighten.

STEP 7. Process the Jars in a Water Bath Canner

Place filled jars on the rack inside your canner, ensuring that they don't touch each other or the sides of the pot. Fill the canner with enough water to cover jars by at least one inch.

Bring water to a rolling boil and start timing according to your recipe's recommended processing time. Maintain a gentle boil throughout the processing period, adding more water if needed.

STEP 8. Cool and Check the Seals

Using a jar lifter, carefully remove the jars from the canner and set them on a towel-covered surface away from direct sunlight. Allow them to cool completely for 12 to 24 hours before checking their seals.

To check, press down on each lid — a properly sealed lid will not move or make any noise when pressed. You can also try lifting each one by its edge using only your fingertips. If a seal is unsuccessful, either refrigerate and consume within two weeks or reprocess using a new lid.

STEP 9. Store Your Preserves

Label your jars with dates and contents, remove screw bands, and store them in a cool, dark place for up to one year.

Following these steps ensures that you'll have flavorful, safely preserved foods ready for consumption all year round! Happy canning!

Chapter 6.　Benefits of Preserving Foods

Apart from the most obvious benefit of canning and preserving your food which is a longer shelf life, there are numerous benefits which include:

*Convenience*It is always convenient to have healthy cooked or near cooked food in your house at all times because it means that a tasty meal is only a few Minuts. away. The convenience of just opening a jar of food and whipping up a quick meal for your family is something most of us would dedicate a weekend to preparing an assortment of canned foods.

*Safety for your Family*The whole world is now grappling with a pandemic (Covid 19) that has turned the world, as we know it, upside down. With people being discouraged from traveling to locations that draw crowds, such as grocery shops, it makes more sense than ever to stock up on food and remains at home, and what better method to guarantee that the food you buy in bulk stays fresh for as long as possible than canning and preserving?

*Budget-Friendly*When going to the market to get food is discouraged and the cost of food has increased, you can save yourself a lot of money by doing bulk shopping and coming home to preserve the food through canning. Additionally, you can also save a lot on buying foods in bulk that are in season and cheap to acquire and can them for extended use and nutrition.

*Controlling every ingredient that goes into your meal*Why not just buy canned food? The answer is quite simple if you want to avoid artificial preservatives and over-processed ingredients, then doing it yourself is the solution. The beauty of self-canning is that you can choose to make your food combinations in a way that makes cooking healthy meals more personalized and ultimately healthy. You will realize that you don't waste any single food item in your can because you know exactly what you used to prepare it in the first place.

*A Well-Stocked Pantry*A pantry that is well stocked translates to variety and fewer hustles of going out to buy your food. Enjoy a great possibility of variety with our simple and fun recipes that make meal time something you look forward to.

*Form of Therapy*Doing something good for you and your friends and family can be very fulfilling and can be a form of therapy for you. The step-by-step procedure is incredibly calming, and knowing that you are doing something that will enhance your health and is long-term will make you feel accomplished and at ease.

Chapter 7.   Tips for Food Safety

Despite the anxiety this information may cause, the best defense against bringing illness into your home is to use your head. Most cases of food poisoning can be avoided by following these food safety guidelines:

- Always use clean hands when working with food, and wipe down your counters and cutting boards as well.
- Rub the entire surface of the vegetables or ingredients with clean hands and rinse under running water. No soap or detergent is required; just rubbing your hands together will release the muck and bacteria it's harboring, and the water will wash it away.
- Do not allow the product to soak. To guarantee that every surface of each berry, bean, or other small food is thoroughly rinsed, use shallow layers of a colander or filter.
- Never, ever, ever let fluid from raw meats, not even little splatters, come into touch with any equipment or utensil that will come into contact with fruits or vegetables, or the fruits and vegetables themselves.
- Wash your hands and any surfaces that touched raw meat or liquids.
- Put your best hygiene foot forward while you're storing food.
- Take the necessary steps to sterilize any equipment or containers that require it.
- Always separate raw, cooked, processed, and unprocessed foods.

The additional steps might appear to require a lot of extra work, time, and effort, but they are minor inconveniences compared to the time and energy spent recovering from a food-borne illness and the cost of possible hospitalization and medication.

Chapter 8.   Frequently Asked Questions

1. If I use a pressure canner, do I have total freedom in developing my preserve recipe?

Answer: If you use a pressure canner, you are limited in how you can create your preserves' recipe. Low-acid foods should only be canned using the pressure canning method. Veggies, meats, poultry, fish, and dairy products are all considered low-acid foods. Food-poisoning bacteria can be found in these products. If you use a canner with boiling water, you can use whatever recipe you like. Processing it in a pressure canner, on the other hand, requires adhering to a tried-and-true recipe.

2. Does a little air inside a homemade canned tomato sauce affect its preservation?

Answer: A little air inside a homemade canned tomato sauce does not affect its preservation. However, if there is too much air in the sauce, it may cause the sauce to spoil. The sauce may become discolored and have off-flavors. To prevent this, leave 1/2-inch headspace when filling jars with tomato sauce.

3. What are some ways of keeping cooked food from spoiling?

Answer: Some ways of keeping cooked food from spoiling are to cook food at the proper temperature, to avoid cross contamination, and to refrigerate food promptly. When food is cooked to the right temperature, dangerous bacteria that can lead to foodborne sickness are eliminated. Avoiding cross contamination helps to prevent the spread of bacteria. Refrigerating or freezing food in an airtight container promptly helps to keep bacteria from growing.

4. If you're canning preserves or applesauce, is it ok to not use a water bath or steam canner and instead just rely on the heat from the food to seal the jar lids, as long as the jars were well washed with hot soapy water before filling them?

Answer: You should not rely on the heat from the food to seal the jar lids when canning preserves or applesauce. Process the jars in a boiling water canner or a pressure canner to ensure the food is secure for consumption.

5. Why did my grandma use wax seals on her homemade fruit preserves? Shouldn't a water bath or a pressure cooker to make it shelf stable work better and have a lower chance of spoilage?

Answer: Your grandma used wax seals on her homemade fruit preserves because that was the best way to seal jars at that time. Sealing jars with wax was a common practice before the invention of the screw-on lid and rubber seal. Wax seals provide an airtight seal that prevents oxygen from entering the jar and causing the food to spoil. Wax seals also help to prevent mold and bacteria from growing on the food. Wax sealing is not required if you are processing the jars in a boiling water canner or pressure canner.

6. What are the best vegetables for canning/preserving?

Answer: The best vegetables for canning and preserving are those that are in season and have a high-water content. Some examples of vegetables that are well suited for canning and preserving are tomatoes, cucumbers, peppers, and squash. These vegetables can be canned or preserved in a variety of ways, including canning in a boiling water canner, pressure canning, pickling, and dehydrating.

7. How is food preserved by canning?

Answer: Food is preserved by canning by sterilizing it in a pressure canner, boiling water canner, or a combination of both. Food is also preserved by pickling in a brine solution or vinegar solution. Canning is the method of preserving food by putting it through a heat treatment in a pressure cooker or a boiling water canner, which is a way of preserving food by packing it into jars while it is hot so that the food doesn't lose any of its nutrients.

8. What food preserved in jars doesn't require canning?

Answer: Pickles, jams, and jellies, which are all food preserved in jars, don't require canning. They are stored in sealed containers and are safe to eat without being processed.

WATER BATH CANNING RECIPES

Chapter 9.   JAM, JELLIES & FRUIT BUTTER

1. Honeyberry Jam Delight

Preparation time: 20 mins

Cooking time: 30 mins

Processing time: 10 mins

Yield: 5 half-pint jars

Ingredients:

- Four cups honeyberries
- One tablespoon lemon juice
- Three cups granulated sugar
- Three tablespoons pectin powder

Directions:

1. Wash honeyberries and remove any debris or damaged berries.
2. Place the honeyberries plus lemon juice in your big non-reactive saucepan, then crush them using your potato masher.
3. Stir in the pectin powder until dissolved. Let it boil on high temp, mixing well. Gradually mix in sugar till it dissolves. Let it boil again within one min while mixing.
4. Remove your saucepan, let it sit for five mins then skim off any foam that has formed.
5. Ladle it into your sanitized jars with quarter" headspace. Wipe jar rims, then secure with lids plus bands. Process jars in your water bath canner within 5 mins.
6. Remove jars from water bath using jar lifters, cool it down within 12-24 hours before checking for proper sealing.

Nutritional Values: Calories: 70; Carbs: 18g; Fat: 0g; Protein: 0g

2. Mandarin Orange Jam

Preparation time: 15 mins

Cooking time: 35 mins

Processing time: 10 mins

Yield: Six 8-ounce jars

Ingredients:

- Eight cups of peeled and chopped mandarin oranges
- Three & half cups of white sugar
- One teaspoon grated lemon zest
- Half a teaspoon unsalted butter
- One package of powdered fruit pectin (1.75 ounces)

Directions:

1. In your big, heavy-bottomed saucepan, mix mandarin oranges, sugar, zest, plus butter. Let it boil on moderate-high temp, mixing frequently.
2. Once it thickens, add powdered fruit pectin, then boil it again for exactly one min, stirring constantly. Remove your saucepan, then scoop any foam on top.
3. Ladle it into your sanitized jars with quarter" headspace. Clean your jar rims, then secure using lids plus bands. Process jars in your water bath canner within 10 mins.
4. Remove jars from water bath using jar lifters, cool it down within 12-24 hours before checking for proper sealing.

Nutritional Values: Calories: 45; Carbs: 11g; Fat: 0g; Protein: 0g

3. Homemade Guava Jam

Preparation time: 30 mins

Cooking time: 20 mins

Processing time: 10 mins

Yield: 4 cups of jam

Ingredients:

- Four cups fresh guava, seeded and chopped
- One & half cups granulated sugar
- One-fourth cup lemon juice
- Half a teaspoon unsalted butter
- Three tablespoons fruit pectin

Directions:

1. In your big saucepan, mix chopped guava, sugar, plus lemon juice. Cook on moderate temp till guava is soft.
2. Add fruit pectin, mix well, let it boil, then adjust to a simmer within 15-20 mins, or until the jam reaches your desired thickness.
3. Stir in the unsalted butter to reduce any foam that may have formed during cooking.
4. Ladle it into your sanitized jars with quarter" headspace. Clean your jar rims, then secure using lids plus bands. Process jars in your water bath canner within 10 mins.
5. Remove jars from water bath using jar lifters, cool it down within 12-24 hours before checking for proper sealing.

Nutritional Values: Calories: 41; Carbs: 10g; Fat: 0g; Protein: 0g

4. Homemade Blackberry Jam

Preparation time: 30 mins

Cooking time: 10 mins

Processing time: 10 mins

Yield: 6 half-pint jars

Ingredients:

- Four cups crushed blackberries
- One tablespoon lemon juice
- Seven cups granulated sugar
- One box (1.75 ounces) powdered fruit pectin
- Half teaspoon butter

Directions:

1. In your big saucepan, mix crushed blackberries, lemon juice, plus pectin. Stir to mix. Let it boil on high temp, mixing well.
2. Put sugar plus butter, stirring until completely dissolved. Let it boil within exactly 1 min, stirring. Remove, let it stand within 5 mins, remove any foam.
3. Ladle it into your sanitized jars with ¼" headspace. Clean your jar rims, then secure with lids plus bands.
4. Process jars in your water bath canner within 10 mins.
5. Carefully remove jars using tongs or jar lifters; let them cool undisturbed on a wire rack or counter before storing.

Nutritional Values: Calories: 56; Carbs: 14g; Fat: 0g; Protein: 0g

5. Pear and Pineapple Jam

Preparation time: 20 mins

Cooking time: 40 mins

Processing time: 10 mins

Yield: 6 half-pint jars

Ingredients:

- Four cups ripe pears, peeled, cored, & chopped
- One cup pineapple, peeled, cored, and chopped
- Two tablespoons lemon juice
- Five cups granulated sugar
- One pinch of cinnamon (optional)
- Half package of powdered fruit pectin (about 1 ounce)

Directions:

1. In your big pot, combine chopped pears plus pineapple. Mix in lemon juice. Gradually put sugar, stirring well to dissolve each addition.
2. Add the powdered fruit pectin and stir until completely dissolved. Let it boil on moderate-high temp, mixing well.
3. Add cinnamon (optional), and continue boiling for another min or until it reaches the jam setting point (220°F).
4. Ladle it into your sanitized jars with 1/4" headspace. Clean your jar rims, then secure with lids plus bands. Process jars in your water bath canner within 10 mins.
5. Remove jars from water bath using jar lifters, cool it down within 12-24 hours before checking for proper sealing.

Nutritional Values: Calories: 40; Carbs: 10g; Fat: 0g; Protein: 0g

6. Classic Blackcurrant Jam

Preparation time: 20 mins

Cooking time: 30 mins

Processing time: 10 mins

Yield: 6 half-pint jars (8 ounces each)

Ingredients:

- Four cups fresh blackcurrants, stemmed and washed
- One tablespoon lemon juice
- Six cups sugar
- One pouch liquid fruit pectin (3 ounces)

Directions:

1. In your big saucepan, mix blackcurrants plus lemon juice. Crush the fruit slightly, then mix in sugar until it dissolves completely.
2. Let it boil within 1 min on moderate-high temp. Mix in liquid pectin, then boil again within 1 min, mixing well.
3. Remove, then let jam cool for five mins, stirring occasionally to redistribute fruit evenly throughout the jam.
4. Ladle it into your sanitized jars with 1/4" headspace. Clean your jar rims, then secure with lids plus bands. Process jars in your water bath canner within 10 mins.
5. Remove jars from water bath using jar lifters, cool it down within 12-24 hours before checking for proper sealing.

Nutritional Values: Calories: 56; Carbs: 14g; Fat: 0g; Protein: 0g

7. Blueberry Vanilla Jam

Preparation time: 15 mins

Cooking time: 30 mins

Processing time: 10 mins

Yield: 8 half-pint jars

Ingredients:

- Four cups fresh blueberries (crushed)
- One tablespoon grated lemon zest
- Three cups granulated sugar
- One tablespoon lemon juice
- One teaspoon pure vanilla extract
- One box fruit pectin

Directions:

1. In your big saucepan, mix crushed blueberries, grated lemon zest, plus lemon juice. Slowly stir in the fruit pectin until well combined.
2. Let it boil on high temp while mixing. Add granulated sugar, then let it boil again while mixing within 1 min. Remove, then stir in vanilla extract. Skim off any foam that may have formed during cooking.
3. Ladle it into your sanitized jars with 1/4" headspace. Clean your jar rims, then secure with lids plus bands. Process jars in your water bath canner within 10 mins.
4. Remove jars from water bath using jar lifters, cool it down within 12-24 hours before checking for proper sealing.

Nutritional Values: Calories: 50; Carbs: 14g; Fat: 0g; Protein: 0g

8. Maple Blackberry Jam

Preparation time: 15 mins

Cooking time: 25 mins

Processing time: 10 mins

Yield: 6 half-pint jars

Ingredients:

- Four cups fresh blackberries
- One cup pure maple syrup
- One tablespoon lemon juice
- One teaspoon calcium water (from Pomona's Pectin)
- Two cups granulated sugar
- Two teaspoons pectin powder (Pomona's Universal Pectin)

Directions:

1. In your big pot, mash blackberries, then mix in maple syrup, lemon juice, plus calcium water.
2. In your container, mix sugar plus pectin powder. Let it boil on moderate-high temp.
3. Slowly mix in sugar-pectin mixture, then let it boil while mixing within 2 mins.

4. Remove, then stir in vanilla extract. Skim off any foam that may have formed during cooking.
5. Ladle it into your sanitized jars with 1/4" headspace. Clean your jar rims, then secure with lids plus bands. Process jars in your water bath canner within 10 mins.
6. Remove jars from water bath using jar lifters, cool it down within 12-24 hours before checking for proper sealing.

Nutritional Values: Calories: 48; Carbs: 12g; Fat: 0g; Protein: 0g

9. Jasmine Tea Jelly

Preparation time: 15 mins

Cooking time: 10 mins

Processing time: 5 mins

Yield: 6 half-pint jars

Ingredients:

- One cup of water
- Four cups of brewed jasmine tea
- Two tablespoons of fresh lemon juice
- One box (1.75 oz) of powdered fruit pectin
- Four and a half cups of granulated sugar

Directions:

1. In your big saucepan, let water plus jasmine tea boil.
2. Add fresh lemon juice, then slowly whisk in powdered fruit pectin. Continue stirring till it boils.
3. Gradually mix in granulated sugar, then let it boil while continuously stirring. Once sugar is dissolved, let the mixture boil within 1 min.
4. Remove your saucepan, let it sit for five mins then skim off any foam that has formed while stirring occasionally.
5. Ladle it into your sanitized jars with 1/4" headspace. Clean your jar rims, then secure with lids plus bands. Process jars in your water bath canner within 5 mins.
6. Remove jars from water bath using jar lifters, cool it down within 12-24 hours before checking for proper sealing.

Nutritional Values: Calories: 45; Carbs: 11g; Fat: 0g; Protein: 0g

10. Spicy Jalapeño Pepper Jelly

Preparation time: 20 mins

Cooking time: 10 mins

Processing time: 10 mins

Yield: 6 half-pint jars

Ingredients:

- Four cups finely chopped jalapeño peppers (about twenty large jalapeños)
- One cup apple cider vinegar
- One (1.75 oz) package of powdered fruit pectin
- Five cups sugar, granulated
- One-fourth cup fresh lime juice
- Salt, as needed

Directions:

1. In your big saucepan, combine jalapeño peppers, apple cider vinegar, powdered fruit pectin, plus salt. Let it boil on high temp, mixing frequently.
2. Add sugar plus fresh lime juice to the saucepan; stir continuously. Let it boil again within one min. Remove your saucepan, then remove any foam on top.
3. Ladle it into your sanitized jars with 1/4" headspace. Clean your jar rims, then secure with lids plus bands. Process jars in your water bath canner within 10 mins.
4. Remove jars from water bath using jar lifters, cool it down within 12-24 hours before checking for proper sealing.

Nutritional Values: Calories: 45; Carbs: 11g; Fat: 0g; Protein: 0g

11. Cranberry Orange Jelly

Preparation time: 15 mins

Cooking time: 10 mins

Processing time: 10 mins

Yield: 6 half-pint jars

Ingredients:

- Four cups fresh cranberries
- Two large oranges, zest and juice
- One tablespoon grated ginger
- Five cups granulated sugar
- One cup water
- One package (1.75 ounces) fruit pectin

Directions:

1. In your big saucepan, mix cranberries, orange zest, orange juice, grated ginger, and water. Cook within 10 mins on moderate temp till it becomes thick.
2. Remove, strain mixture into your bowl, then discard solids. Put strained mixture to your saucepan, then mix in till it dissolves.
3. Let it boil on high temp, mixing well. Add fruit pectin and continue boiling for another min. Remove your saucepan, then remove any foam on top.
4. Ladle it into your sanitized jars with 1/4" headspace. Clean your jar rims, then secure with lids plus bands. Process jars in your water bath canner within 10 mins.
5. Remove jars from water bath using jar lifters, cool it down within 12-24 hours before checking for proper sealing.

Nutritional Values: Calories: 48; Carbs: 12g; Fat: 0g; Protein: 0g

12. Apple Kiwi Jelly

Preparation time: 20 mins

Cooking time: 10 mins

Processing time: 10 mins

Yield: 6 half-pint jars

Ingredients:

- Five cups finely chopped apples
- Four cups finely chopped kiwis
- Three cups granulated sugar
- One and a half cups water
- Quarter cup lemon juice
- Half a teaspoon of unsalted butter
- One package (1.75 ounces) powdered fruit pectin

Directions:

1. In your big saucepan, mix chopped apples, kiwis, water, plus lemon juice. Cook within 10 mins on moderate temp till fruit is softened.
2. Stir in sugar until dissolved, then add the butter. Let it boil on high temp, mixing well.
3. Quickly add the powdered fruit pectin, then let it boil within one min, mixing to avoid sticking. Remove your saucepan, then remove any foam on top.
4. Ladle it into your sanitized jars with 1/4" headspace. Clean your jar rims, then secure with lids plus bands. Process jars in your water bath canner within 10 mins.
5. Remove jars from water bath using jar lifters, cool it down within 12-24 hours before checking for proper sealing and storing.

Nutritional Values: Calories: 15; Carbs: 3g; Fat: 0g; Protein: <1g

13. Homemade Cucumber Jelly

Preparation time: 15 mins

Cooking time: 10 mins

Processing time: 10 mins

Yield: 4 (8-ounce) jars

Ingredients:

- Two cups cucumber, peeled, seeded, and finely chopped
- One & half cups granulated sugar
- One half cup white vinegar
- One quarter cup water
- One tablespoon freshly squeezed lemon juice

- Two teaspoons fruit pectin

Directions:

1. In your medium-sized saucepan, mix chopped cucumber, sugar, vinegar, water, plus lemon juice. Mix well.
2. Let it boil on moderate-high temp, mixing till sugar dissolves. Once boiling, add the fruit pectin, then boil again within 1 min while mixing continuously.
3. Remove your saucepan, then remove any foam on top.
4. Ladle it into your sanitized jars with 1/4" headspace. Clean your jar rims, then secure with lids plus bands. Process jars in your water bath canner within 10 mins.
5. Remove jars from water bath using jar lifters, cool it down within 12-24 hours before checking for proper sealing and storing.

Nutritional Values: Calories: 60; Carbs: 15g; Fat: 0g; Protein: 0g

14. Sweet and Spicy Bell Pepper Jelly

Preparation time: 20 mins

Cooking time: 20 mins

Processing time: 10 mins

Yield: 8-10 half-pint jars

Ingredients:

- Four large bell peppers (red, yellow, orange, and green), finely chopped
- Two cups apple cider vinegar
- Six cups sugar, granulated
- One-half teaspoon crushed red pepper flakes
- One quarter teaspoon salt
- One pouch liquid pectin (three ounces)

Directions:

1. In your big saucepan, mix finely chopped bell peppers, apple cider vinegar, granulated sugar, crushed red pepper flakes, and salt. Let it boil on high temp while mixing within 10 mins till sugar is fully dissolved.
2. Add liquid pectin, then mix well. Boil it again within 4-5 mins, until it reaches a thicker consistency. Remove your saucepan, then remove any foam on top.
3. Ladle it into your sanitized jars with one-fourth" headspace. Clean your jar rims, then secure with lids plus bands. Process jars in your water bath canner within 10 mins.
4. Remove jars from water bath using jar lifters, cool it down within 12-24 hours before checking for proper sealing and storing.

Nutritional Values: Calories: 42; Carbs: 10g; Fat: 0g; Protein: 0g

15. Watermelon Jelly

Preparation time: 20 mins

Cooking time: 10 mins

Processing time: 15 mins

Yield: Six half-pint jars

Ingredients:

- Four cups watermelon puree, seeds removed
- One and a half cups granulated sugar
- One cup white grape juice
- One package powdered fruit pectin (one point seven five ounces)
- Three tablespoons lemon juice

Directions:

1. In your big saucepan, mix watermelon puree, sugar, plus white grape juice. Slowly stir in powdered fruit pectin.
2. Let it boil on high temp while mixing. Once boiling, continue to boil within 1 min, then remove your saucepan. Mix in lemon juice. Remove your saucepan, then remove any foam on top.
3. Ladle it into your sanitized jars with one-fourth" headspace. Clean your jar rims, then secure with lids plus bands. Process jars in your water bath canner within 15 mins.
4. Remove jars from water bath using jar lifters, cool it down within 12-24 hours before checking for proper sealing and storing.

Nutritional Values: Calories: 105; Carbs: 27g; Fat: 0g; Protein: 0g

16. Raspberry Blueberry Jelly

Preparation time: 20 mins

Cooking time: 15 mins

Processing time: 10 mins

Yield: 6 half-pint jars

Ingredients:

- Four cups raspberries
- Four cups blueberries
- One cup water
- Seven cups granulated sugar
- One package (1.75 ounces) fruit pectin, no sugar needed

Directions:

1. Mix raspberries, blueberries, plus water in your big saucepan on moderate temp. Simmer within 5 mins till berries are softened and have released their juice. Strain berry mixture into your big pot, pressing the solids.
2. In your big container, mix sugar plus pectin. Return your pot with strained juice to moderate temp, then gradually mix in sugar-pectin mixture till completely dissolved.

3. Let it boil within 1 min while mixing. Remove your saucepan, then remove any foam on top.
4. Ladle it into your sanitized jars with 1/4" headspace. Clean your jar rims, then secure with lids plus bands. Process jars in your water bath canner within 10 mins.
5. Remove jars from water bath using jar lifters, cool it down within 12-24 hours before checking for proper sealing and storing.

Nutritional Values: Calories: 53; Carbs: 13g; Fat: 0g; Protein: 0g

17. Blackberry Apple Jelly

Preparation time: 30 mins

Cooking time: 20 mins

Processing time: 10 mins

Yield: About 6 half-pint jars

Ingredients:

- Four cups fresh blackberries
- Four cups chopped apples, peeled & cored
- One cup water
- Two tablespoons lemon juice
- Five cups sugar
- One (1.75 oz) package fruit pectin

Directions:

1. In your big pot, mix blackberries, apples, plus water. Let it boil on moderate-high temp, then adjust to a simmer within 20 mins till fruit is soft.
2. Using a fine-mesh sieve or jelly bag, strain the cooked fruit, collecting the juice in your container. Discard any pulp.
3. Measure out five cups of fruit juice and place it in your big pot with lemon juice. Mix in pectin, then let it heat on rolling boil on high temp, mixing constantly.
4. Mix in sugar all at once, then let it heat again on full rolling boil within 1 min. Remove your saucepan, then remove any foam on top.
5. Ladle it into your sanitized jars with 1/4" headspace. Clean your jar rims, then secure with lids plus bands. Process jars in your water bath canner within 10 mins.
6. Remove jars from water bath using jar lifters, cool it down within 12-24 hours before checking for proper sealing and storing.

Nutritional Values: Calories: 56; Carbs: 14g; Fat: 0g; Protein: 0g

18. Caramel Apple Butter

Preparation time: 30 minutes

Cooking time: 1 hour & 30 minutes

Processing time: 25 minutes

Yield: 6 pint jars

Ingredients:

- 5 pounds apples, peeled, cored& and chopped
- 2 cups granulated sugar
- 1 cup brown sugar
- 1 tablespoon ground cinnamon
- 1/2 teaspoon ground nutmeg
- 1/4 teaspoon ground cloves
- 1 cup water
- 1/2 cup apple cider vinegar
- 1 teaspoon pure vanilla extract

Directions:

1. In your big pot, mix apples, granulated sugar, brown sugar, cinnamon, nutmeg, cloves, water, plus apple cider vinegar.
2. Let it boil on moderate-high temp. Adjust to low temp, then simmer within 1 hour till apples are soft. Puree cooked apples using your immersion blender till smooth. Add vanilla, then mix well.
3. Ladle it into your sanitized jars with 1/4" headspace. Clean your jar rims, then secure with lids plus bands. Process jars in your water bath canner within 25 mins.
4. Remove jars from water bath using jar lifters, cool it down within 12-24 hours before checking for proper sealing and storing.

Nutritional Values: Calories: 24; Carbs: 6g; Fat: 0g; Protein: 0g

19. Lavender Apricot Butter

Preparation time: 20 mins

Cooking time: 1 hour

Processing time: 15 mins

Yield: About 6 half-pint jars

Ingredients:

- Four cups quartered, pitted fresh apricots (approximately twenty-four apricots)
- One tablespoon dried culinary lavender
- Two and a half cups granulated sugar
- Two tablespoons freshly squeezed lemon juice

Directions:

1. In your big non-reactive saucepan, mix apricots plus lavender. Cook within 15-20 mins on moderate temp, mixing often till apricots are easily mashed.
2. Blend apricot-lavender mixture using your immersion blender till smooth. Add sugar plus lemon juice, then mix well.
3. Cook within 45 mins on moderate-low temp, mixing often till butter has thickened.
4. Ladle it into your sanitized jars with 1/4" headspace. Clean your jar rims, then secure with lids plus bands. Process jars in your water bath canner within 15 mins.
5. Remove jars from water bath using jar lifters, cool it down within 12-24 hours before checking for proper sealing and storing.

Nutritional Values: Calories: 43; Carbs: 11g; Fat: 0g; Protein: 0.2g

20. Blueberry Cherry Butter

Preparation time: 20 mins

Cooking time: 1 hour

Processing time: 20 mins

Yield: Five half-pint jars (8 ounces each)

Ingredients:

- Four cups fresh blueberries
- Three cups pitted and chopped fresh cherries
- One and a half cups sugar, granulated
- One tablespoon lemon juice, fresh
- Half tablespoon grated lemon zest

Directions:

1. Mix blueberries, cherries, sugar, lemon juice, plus lemon zest in your big saucepan. Cook on moderate temp till sugar dissolves, stirring occasionally.
2. Adjust to a simmer within one hour till it thickens. Remove, then cool it down. Puree mixture using your immersion blender till smooth.
3. Ladle it into your sanitized jars with 1/4" headspace. Clean your jar rims, then secure with lids plus bands. Process jars in your water bath canner within 20 mins.
4. Remove jars from water bath using jar lifters, cool it down within 12-24 hours before checking for proper sealing and storing.

Nutritional Values: Calories: 90; Carbs: 23g; Fat: 0g; Protein: 0g

21. Cinnamon Apple Butter

Preparation time: 30 mins

Cooking time: 2 hours

Processing time: 10 mins

Yield: 8 cups

Ingredients:

- Twenty medium apples, peeled, cored, and sliced
- Two cups granulated sugar
- Three-quarters cup packed brown sugar
- One tablespoon cinnamon, ground
- One teaspoon allspice, ground
- Half teaspoon cloves, ground
- Half teaspoon salt

Directions:

1. In your big pot, mix apples, granulated sugar, brown sugar, cinnamon, allspice, cloves, plus salt.
2. Cook within 45 mins on moderate temp till apples are tender, mixing often. Puree mixture using your immersion blender till smooth.
3. Simmer on low temp within 1 hour and 15 mins till thickened. Ladle it into your sanitized jars with 1/4" headspace.
4. Clean your jar rims, then secure with lids plus bands. Process jars in your water bath canner within 10 mins.
5. Remove jars from water bath using jar lifters, cool it down within 12-24 hours before checking for proper sealing and storing.

Nutritional Values: Calories: 40; Carbs: 10g; Fat: 0g; Protein: 0g

22. Plum Mandarin Butter

Preparation time: 30 mins

Cooking time: 1 hour

Processing time: 10 mins

Yield: 6 half-pint jars

Ingredients:

- Three pounds plums, pitted and quartered
- One cup granulated sugar
- One cup water
- Three mandarin oranges, juiced and zested
- One tablespoon fresh lemon juice
- One teaspoon cinnamon, ground
- Half a teaspoon ginger, ground

Directions:

1. Mix plums, sugar, and water in your big heavy-bottomed pot on moderate temp; mixing till sugar dissolved.
2. Mix in mandarin juice, zest, lemon juice, cinnamon, and ginger to the pot. Simmer on low heat within an hour till it reaches a thick, jam-like consistency. Be sure to stir occasionally to prevent sticking or burning.
3. Simmer on low temp within 1 hour and 15 mins till thickened. Ladle it into your sanitized jars with 1/4" headspace.
4. Clean your jar rims, then secure with lids plus bands. Process jars in your water bath canner within 10 mins.
5. Remove jars from water bath using jar lifters, cool it down within 12-24 hours before checking for proper sealing and storing.

Nutritional Values: Calories: 120; Carbs: 25g; Fat: 0g; Protein: 1g

23. Golden Fruit Butter

Preparation time: 30 mins

Cooking time: 1 hour & 15 mins

Processing time: 10 mins

Yield: 6 half-pint jars

Ingredients:

- Four cups chopped mixed fruit (peaches, apricots, pears, plums)
- One and a half cups granulated sugar
- One tablespoon lemon zest, grated
- Two tablespoons lemon juice, fresh
- One teaspoon cinnamon, ground
- Half teaspoon nutmeg, ground
- Quarter teaspoon salt

Directions:

1. In your big deep saucepan, mix chopped mixed fruit, granulated sugar, lemon zest, and lemon juice. Stir well to mix.
2. Put your saucepan on moderate temp, then cook till sugar dissolves completely, stirring occasionally to prevent sticking.
3. Adjust to low temp, then cook within 1 hour or until it reaches a butter-like consistency. Stir occasionally to prevent burning. Add ground cinnamon, ground nutmeg, plus salt. Mix well.
4. Ladle it into your sanitized jars with 1/4" headspace. Clean your jar rims, then secure with lids plus bands. Process jars in your water bath canner within 10 mins.
5. Remove jars from water bath using jar lifters, cool it down within 12-24 hours before checking for proper sealing and storing.

Nutritional Values: Calories: 40; Carbs: 10g; Fat: 0g; Protein: 0g

24. Peachy Keen Butter

Preparation time: 30 mins

Cooking time: 1 hour

Processing time: 20 mins

Yield: 4-pint jars

Ingredients:

- Four pounds fresh peaches, peeled, pitted, & chopped
- One cup granulated sugar
- Two tablespoons fresh lemon juice
- Half teaspoon cinnamon, ground

- Quarter teaspoon nutmeg, ground

Directions:

1. In your big saucepan, mix chopped peaches, sugar, lemon juice, cinnamon, plus nutmeg. Cook mixture on moderate temp, mixing often till sugar has dissolved.
2. Let it boil gently. Adjust to a simmer within an hour till it reaches desired thickness. Stir occasionally to prevent sticking.
3. Ladle it into your sanitized jars with 1/4" headspace. Clean your jar rims, then secure with lids plus bands. Process jars in your water bath canner within 20 mins.
4. Remove jars from water bath using jar lifters, cool it down within 12-24 hours before checking for proper sealing and storing.

Nutritional Values: Calories: 30; Carbs: 26g; Fat: 0g; Protein: 0g

25. Vanilla Pear Butter

Preparation time: 20 mins

Cooking time: 2 hours

Processing time: 15 mins

Yield: 6 (8-ounce) jars

Ingredients:

- Eight cups chopped ripe pears
- One cup granulated sugar
- Two tablespoons fresh lemon juice
- One tablespoon pure vanilla extract

Directions:

1. In your big heavy-bottomed pot, mix chopped pears, sugar, plus lemon juice. Let it boil on moderate-high temp, stirring occasionally.
2. Adjust to low temp, then simmer within one hour, mixing often till pears are soft. Blend using your immersion blender till smooth.
3. Mix in vanilla extract, then cook on low temp within 1 hour till mixture thickens.
4. Ladle it into your sanitized jars with 1/4" headspace. Clean your jar rims, then secure with lids plus bands. Process jars in your water bath canner within 15 mins.
5. Remove jars from water bath using jar lifters, cool it down within 12-24 hours before checking for proper sealing and storing.

Nutritional Values: Calories: 37; Carbs: 9g; Fat: 0g; Protein: 0g

Chapter 10. MARMALADE & PRESERVES

26. Prickly Pear Cactus Marmalade

Preparation time: 30 mins

Cooking time: 40 mins

Processing time: 10 mins

Yield: About 5 half-pint jars

Ingredients:

- Three cups prickly pear cactus juice, strained
- One and a half cups freshly squeezed orange juice, with pulp
- Two tablespoons lemon juice
- Six cups granulated sugar
- One package fruit pectin, either powdered or liquid
- Half a cup seedless raisin
- One tablespoon grated orange zest

Directions:

1. In your big saucepan, mix prickly pear cactus juice, orange & lemon juice, plus sugar. Let it boil gently on moderate temp while continuously stirring.
2. Add the fruit pectin and continue to stir until it is completely dissolved into the mixture.
3. Keeping the mixture at a rolling boil, add the raisins and orange zest, stirring occasionally for another five mins or until the marmalade reaches your desired consistency.
4. Remove, then skim off any foam that may have formed during cooking.
5. Ladle it into your sanitized jars with 1/4" headspace. Clean your jar rims, then secure with lids plus bands. Process jars in your water bath canner within 10 mins.
6. Remove jars from water bath using jar lifters, cool it down within 12-24 hours before checking for proper sealing and storing.

Nutritional Values: Calories: 86; Carbs: 22g; Fat: 0g; Protein: 0g

27. Rhubarb Raisin Marmalade

Preparation time: 20 mins

Cooking time: 30 mins

Processing time: 10 mins

Yield: 4 half-pint jars

Ingredients:

- Four cups chopped fresh rhubarb
- One and a half cups golden raisins
- Two and a half cups sugar
- One tablespoon grated orange zest
- One tablespoon grated lemon zest
- Half a cup fresh orange juice
- Quarter cup fresh lemon juice

Directions:

1. In your big heavy pot, mix rhubarb, raisins, sugar, plus all zest. Cook on moderate temp, mixing often till sugar has dissolved.
2. Add all juices, let it boil, then simmer within 25 to 30 mins till it thickens, stirring occasionally to prevent sticking.
3. Remove, then skim off any foam that may have formed during cooking.
4. Ladle it into your sanitized jars with 1/4" headspace. Clean your jar rims, then secure with lids plus bands. Process jars in your water bath canner within 10 mins.
5. Remove jars from water bath using jar lifters, cool it down within 12-24 hours before checking for proper sealing and storing.

Nutritional Values: Calories: 110; Carbs: 26g; Fat: 0g; Protein: 0g

28. Lemon Lime Marmalade

Preparation time: 20 mins

Cooking time: 40 mins

Processing time: 10 mins

Yield: 8 eight-ounce jars

Ingredients:

- Two and a half cups of water
- One and a half cups of fresh lemon juice
- One and a half cups of fresh lime juice
- Two tablespoons lemon zest
- Two tablespoons lime zest
- Six cups granulated sugar

- One-quarter teaspoon ground ginger
- One pack (1.75 ounces) pectin

Directions:

1. In your big pot, mix water, all juices plus zests.
2. In your medium container, thoroughly mix sugar plus ground ginger. Add it to your pot while mixing till it dissolves. Let it boil on high temp, mixing well.
3. Add pectin and continue to cook at a rolling boil for an additional min while stirring. Remove, then skim off any foam that may have formed during cooking.
4. Ladle it into your sanitized jars with 1/4" headspace. Clean your jar rims, then secure with lids plus bands. Process jars in your water bath canner within 10 mins.
5. Remove jars from water bath using jar lifters, cool it down within 12-24 hours before checking for proper sealing and storing.

Nutritional Values: Calories: 56; Carbs: 14g; Fat: 0g; Protein: 0g

29. Blood Orange Marmalade

Preparation time: 40 mins

Cooking time: 20 mins

Processing time: 10 mins

Yield: 6 half-pint jars

Ingredients:

- Six blood oranges
- One and a half cups of granulated sugar
- Three cups of water
- Two tablespoons of freshly squeezed lemon juice
- One-fourth teaspoon of vanilla extract

Directions:

1. Wash, dry, and thinly slice the blood oranges, discarding any seeds.
2. In your big, non-reactive pot, mix sliced blood oranges, sugar, water, and lemon juice. Stir until the sugar has dissolved.
3. Let it boil on moderate-high temp, adjust to low temp, then simmer within 20 mins till marmalade has thickened. Remove your pot, then mix in vanilla extract.

4. Ladle it into your sanitized jars with 1/4" headspace. Clean your jar rims, then secure with lids plus bands. Process jars in your water bath canner within 10 mins.
5. Remove jars from water bath using jar lifters, cool it down within 12-24 hours before checking for proper sealing and storing.

Nutritional Values: Calories: 40; Carbs: 10g; Fat: 0g; Protein: 0g

30. Blueberry Marmalade

Preparation time: 20 mins

Cooking time: 40 mins

Processing time: 15 mins

Yield: 6 to 8 half-pint jars

Ingredients:

- Four cups fresh blueberries, crushed
- One large orange, finely chopped (skin included)
- Two tablespoons grated lemon zest
- One tablespoon lemon juice
- Six cups granulated sugar
- One half teaspoon unsalted butter
- One pouch liquid fruit pectin

Directions:

1. In your big, heavy-bottomed saucepan, mix crushed blueberries, chopped orange, lemon zest, and lemon juice.
2. Gradually stir in the sugar on moderate temp till sugar dissolved. Mix in butter.
3. Let it boil while mixing, add liquid pectin, then gently boil within 1 min while mixing. Remove, then skim off any foam that may have formed during cooking.
4. Ladle it into your sanitized jars with 1/4" headspace. Clean your jar rims, then secure with lids plus bands. Process jars in your water bath canner within 5 mins.
5. Remove jars from water bath using jar lifters, cool it down within 12-24 hours before checking for proper sealing and storing.

Nutritional Values: Calories: 55; Carbs: 14g; Fat: 0g; Protein: 0g

31. Carrot Citrus Marmalade

Preparation time: 20 mins

Cooking time: 25 mins

Processing time: 10 mins

Yield: 6 half-pint jars

Ingredients:

- Two cups of finely grated carrots

- One cup of orange juice
- Half a cup of lemon juice
- Four cups of granulated sugar
- One tablespoon of grated orange zest
- One tablespoon of grated lemon zest
- Half a teaspoon of kosher salt

Directions:

1. In your big, non-reactive saucepan, mix grated carrots, orange juice, lemon juice, granulated sugar, orange zest, lemon zest, and kosher salt.
2. Let it boil on moderate-high temp, stirring frequently till sugar dissolved. Adjust to a simmer within 25 mins till mixture thickens. Make sure to stir occasionally while it's cooking.
3. Remove, then skim off any foam that may have formed during cooking.
4. Ladle mixture into your sanitized jars with 1/4" headspace. Clean your jar rims, then secure with lids plus bands. Process jars in your water bath canner within 10 mins.
5. Remove jars from water bath using jar lifters, cool it down within 12-24 hours before checking for proper sealing and storing.

Nutritional Values: Calories: 40; Carbs: 10g; Fat: 0g; Protein: 0g

32. Lemon Grapefruit Marmalade

Preparation time: 20 mins

Cooking time: 40 mins

Processing time: 10 mins

Yield: 5 cups

Ingredients:

- Two large grapefruits
- One large lemon
- Four and a half cups granulated sugar
- One cup water
- Half a teaspoon unsalted butter

Directions:

1. Thoroughly wash the grapefruits and lemon. Peel grapefruits and lemon using your zester, ensuring you only remove the outer colored part and avoiding the white pith.
2. Slice the zested grapefruits and lemon in half and remove the seeds. In your blender, pulse grapefruits plus lemon till finely chopped.
3. In your big saucepan, mix chopped fruit, zest, sugar, plus water. Cook on moderate temp, stirring occasionally, till sugar dissolves.
4. Add butter to reduce foaming and continue cooking within 40 mins. Remove, then skim off any foam that may have formed during cooking.

5. Ladle mixture into your sanitized jars with 1/4" headspace. Clean your jar rims, then secure with lids plus bands. Process jars in your water bath canner within 10 mins.
6. Remove jars from water bath using jar lifters, cool it down within 12-24 hours before checking for proper sealing and storing.

Nutritional Values: Calories: 55; Carbs: 14g; Fat: 0g; Protein: 0g

33. Vanilla Plum Preserves

Preparation time: 20 mins

Cooking time: 45 mins

Processing time: 10 mins

Yield: 5 half-pint jars

Ingredients:

- Three pounds ripe plums, pitted and chopped
- Two cups granulated sugar
- One and a half teaspoons vanilla extract
- One lemon, juiced and zested
- Two tablespoons no/low-sugar needed pectin

Directions:

1. Combine prepared plums and sugar in your big saucepan. Put your saucepan on moderate temp, then cook till it gently boils; mixing well.
2. Mix in vanilla extract plus lemon juice. Gradually add pectin while mixing. Let it boil gently within 2 mins before removing it from heat.
3. Ladle mixture into your sanitized jars with 1/4" headspace. Clean your jar rims, then secure with lids plus bands. Process jars in your water bath canner within 10 mins.
4. Remove jars from water bath using jar lifters, cool it down within 12-24 hours before checking for proper sealing and storing.

Nutritional Values: Calories: 40; Carbs: 10g; Fat: 0g; Protein: 0g

34. Peach Honey Preserves

Preparation time: 30 mins

Cooking time: 40 mins

Processing time: 15 mins

Yield: 6 half-pint jars

Ingredients:

- Four pounds fresh peaches
- One & half cups pure honey
- One-quarter cup freshly squeezed lemon juice
- One-half teaspoon ground cinnamon

Directions:

1. Peel your peaches by placing them in your pot with boiling water for a min, followed by an ice bath. The skins should slip off easily. Pit, halve, and roughly chop the peeled peaches.
2. In your big heavy-bottomed pot, mix chopped peaches, honey, lemon juice, and cinnamon.
3. Cook over medium heat within 40 mins, stirring frequently to prevent sticking. Cook until the preserves thickens and reaches your desired consistency.
4. Ladle mixture into your sanitized jars with 1/4" headspace. Clean your jar rims, then secure with lids plus bands. Process jars in your water bath canner within 15 mins.
5. Remove jars from water bath using jar lifters, cool it down within 12-24 hours before checking for proper sealing and storing.

Nutritional Values: Calories: 30; Carbs: 8g; Fat: 0g; Protein: 0g

35. Pineapple Lime Preserves

Preparation time: 20 mins

Cooking time: 30 mins

Processing time: 15 mins

Yield: 6 half-pint jars

Ingredients:

- Four cups fresh pineapple, finely chopped
- One and a half cups granulated sugar
- One tablespoon lime zest, finely grated
- Half cup freshly squeezed lime juice
- Half teaspoon unsalted butter

Directions:

1. In your big, non-reactive saucepan, mix chopped pineapple, sugar, lime zest, plus lime juice. Mix well to dissolve sugar.
2. Add butter, then mix on moderate temp it comes to a rolling boil. Cook the preserves within 30 mins until it thickens, stirring occasionally to prevent sticking.
3. Remove, then skim off any foam that may have formed during cooking.
4. Ladle mixture into your sanitized jars with 1/4" headspace. Clean your jar rims, then secure with lids plus bands. Process jars in your water bath canner within 15 mins.
5. Remove jars from water bath using jar lifters, cool it down within 12-24 hours before checking for proper sealing and storing.

Nutritional Values: Calories: 45; Carbs: 11g; Fat: 0g; Protein: 0g

Chapter 11.   PICKLES

36. Curry Cauliflower Pickles

Preparation time: 20 mins

Cooking time: 10 mins

Processing time: 15 mins

Yield: 4 pint jars

Ingredients:

- One medium head of cauliflower, cut into small florets
- Two cups white vinegar
- Two cups water
- One cup granulated sugar
- Half cup kosher salt
- One tablespoon curry powder
- One teaspoon whole mustard seeds
- Four whole garlic cloves, peeled
- Four small fresh chili peppers

Directions:

1. In your big pot, let water plus vinegar boil. Add sugar, salt, curry powder, plus mustard seeds, mixing well. Add cauliflower florets, then simmer within 5 mins till slightly tender.
2. Meanwhile, put one garlic clove plus one chili pepper in each sterilized pint jar. Distribute cauliflower evenly among each.
3. Pour hot pickling liquid with 1/4" headspace. Clean your jar rims, then secure with lids plus bands. Process jars in your water bath canner within 15 mins.
4. Remove jars from water bath using jar lifters, cool it down within 12-24 hours before checking for proper sealing and storing.

Nutritional Values: Calories: 80; Carbs: 18g; Fat: 0g; Protein: 3g

37. Asparagus Pickles

Preparation time: 30 mins

Cooking time: 10 mins

Processing time: 20 mins

Yield: 6 pint jars

Ingredients:

- Three pounds fresh asparagus, trimmed
- Six cups white vinegar
- Three cups water
- One cup granulated sugar
- Two tablespoons pickling salt
- One tablespoon black peppercorns, crushed
- One tablespoon mustard seeds
- Six cloves garlic, thinly sliced
- Six sprigs fresh dill

Directions:

1. Put asparagus into your sterilized jars with ½" headspace.
2. In your big saucepan, mix vinegar, water, sugar, salt, peppercorns, plus mustard seeds. Let it boil on high temp, then adjust to a simmer within 10 mins.
3. Meanwhile, place one sliced garlic clove and one sprig of dill into each clean pint jar. Pack the asparagus tightly into the jars, making sure to maintain the half-inch headspace.
4. Using a ladle or measuring cup with a pour spout, carefully pour hot pickling liquid over asparagus with ½" headspace. Remove any air bubbles using your bubble remover tool.
5. Clean your jar rims, then secure with lids plus bands. Process jars in your water bath canner within 20 mins.
6. Remove jars from water bath using jar lifters, cool it down within 12-24 hours before checking for proper sealing and storing.

Nutritional Values: Calories: 20; Carbs: 4g; Fat: 0g; Protein: 1g

38. Green Beans Pickles

Preparation time: 20 mins

Cooking time: 5 mins

Processing time: 10 mins

Yield: 8 pint jars

Ingredients:

- Twelve pounds of fresh green beans, trimmed and halved to fit the size of the jar
- Eight cups white vinegar
- Eight cups water
- Two-thirds cup pickling salt
- Sixteen cloves of peeled garlic

- One teaspoon red pepper flakes (optional)
- Eight heads fresh dill or sixteen teaspoons of dill seeds

Directions:

1. In your big pot, mix white vinegar, water, plus pickling salt. Let it boil.
2. While the pickling solution is boiling, pack each jar with an equal amount of green beans.
3. Add two cloves of garlic, quarter tsp red pepper flakes (if using), plus one head of fresh dill to each jar.
4. Ladle hot pickling solution into each jar, covering the beans with ½" headspace. Remove any air bubbles using your bubble remover tool.
5. Clean your jar rims, then secure with lids plus bands. Process jars in your water bath canner within 10 mins.
6. Remove jars from water bath using jar lifters, cool it down within 12-24 hours before checking for proper sealing and storing.

Nutritional Values: Calories: 60; Carbs: 11g; Fat: 0g; Protein: 2g

39. Tangy Eggplant Pickles

Preparation time: 20 mins

Cooking time: 10 mins

Processing time: 15 mins

Yield: 6 pints

Ingredients:

- Two pounds of eggplants, sliced into half-inch rounds
- One tablespoon of salt
- Four cups of white vinegar
- One cup of water
- Two cups of granulated sugar
- One teaspoon of mustard seeds
- Half a teaspoon of celery seeds
- Quarter teaspoon of ground turmeric
- Three cloves of garlic, minced

Directions:

1. Rinse the eggplant slices and place them in your big container. Flavor with salt, then let it sit within an hour. This will help extract any bitterness from the eggplants.
2. While the eggplants are sitting, prepare the canning jars by sanitizing them in boiling water.
3. In your big saucepan, mix vinegar, water, sugar, mustard & celery seeds, ground turmeric, plus minced garlic. Let it boil, mixing often till sugar dissolves. Adjust to a simmer within 5 mins.
4. Drain eggplants and rinse them well under running cold water. Pat them dry using your kitchen towel.
5. Add eggplant slices to your vinegar mixture, then cook within 4 to 5 mins till tender.

6. Using a slotted spoon or tongs, pack the hot eggplant slices into prepared jars, leaving half an inch of headspace at the top.
7. Ladle hot pickling liquid over eggplants in jars until they are completely covered. Remove any air bubbles using your bubble remover tool.
8. Clean your jar rims, then secure with lids plus bands. Process jars in your water bath canner within 15 mins.
9. Remove jars from water bath using jar lifters, cool it down within 12-24 hours before checking for proper sealing and storing.

Nutritional Values: Calories: 30; Carbs: 6g; Fat: 0g; Protein: 1g

40. Mushroom Pickles

Preparation time: 20 mins

Cooking time: 10 mins

Processing time: 15 mins

Yield: 4 pint jars

Ingredients:

- Four pounds of small fresh mushrooms, trimmed and cleaned
- Two cups apple cider vinegar
- Two cups water
- One tablespoon of salt
- One tablespoon of whole black peppercorns
- Four teaspoons of dried dill weed
- Four cloves of garlic, minced
- Half a cup of sliced onions

Directions:

1. In your big saucepan, mix apple cider vinegar, water, plus salt. Let it boil. Add mushrooms, then simmer within 5 mins.
2. Meanwhile, place 1/4 tablespoon of whole black peppercorns, 1 teaspoon of dried dill weed, and a minced garlic clove in each pint jar. Add cooked mushrooms with 1" headspace. Divide sliced onions among each.
3. Carefully ladle hot vinegar mixture over mushrooms in each jar to cover them completely with ½" headspace. Remove any air bubbles using your bubble remover tool.

4. Clean your jar rims, then secure with lids plus bands. Process jars in your water bath canner within 15 mins.
5. Remove jars from water bath using jar lifters, cool it down within 12-24 hours before checking for proper sealing and storing.

Nutritional Values: Calories: 72; Carbs: 9g; Fat: 0.5g; Protein: 6g

41. Vinegar Carrot with Dill Pickles

Preparation time: 20 mins

Cooking time: 10 mins

Processing time: 10 mins

Yield: 4 pint jars

Ingredients:

- Four cups thinly-sliced carrots
- Two cups white vinegar
- One & half cups water
- One cup granulated sugar
- Half a cup thinly-sliced onion
- Six cloves garlic, peeled and halved
- Four teaspoons dill seeds
- Four bay leaves

Directions:

1. In your big saucepan, mix vinegar, water, plus sugar. Let it boil, then adjust to a simmer within 5 mins.
2. Divide carrots, onion, garlic cloves, dill seeds, plus bay leaves in your sterilized jars. Pour hot vinegar mixture over the vegetables in each jar with ½" headspace. Remove any air bubbles using your bubble remover tool.
3. Clean your jar rims, then secure with lids plus bands. Process jars in your water bath canner within 10 mins.
4. Remove jars from water bath using jar lifters, cool it down within 12-24 hours before checking for proper sealing and storing.

Nutritional Values: Calories: 98; Carbs: 19g; Fat: 0.2g; Protein: 1g

42. Pickled Brussels Sprouts

Preparation time: 20 mins

Cooking time: 10 mins

Processing time: 15 mins

Yield: 6 pint jars

Ingredients:

- Three pounds of Brussels sprouts, trimmed and halved
- Six cups of white vinegar
- Six cups of water
- One cup of white sugar
- Two tablespoons of kosher salt
- Six cloves of garlic, peeled and halved
- Three teaspoons of crushed red pepper flakes
- One & half teaspoons of mustard seeds
- One & half teaspoons of black peppercorns

Directions:

1. In your big saucepan, mix white vinegar, water, white sugar, plus kosher salt. Let it boil on high temp, stirring occasionally till sugar dissolves. Adjust to low temp, then simmer within 10 mins.
2. Place one clove of halved garlic, half tsp crushed red pepper flakes, a quarter tsp mustard seeds, plus quarter tsp black peppercorns into each sanitized jar.
3. Pack the trimmed and halved Brussels sprouts into your jars with ½" headspace. Ladle the hot pickling liquid into each jar over the Brussels sprouts with ½" headspace.
4. Remove any air bubbles using your bubble remover tool.
5. Clean your jar rims, then secure with lids plus bands. Process jars in your water bath canner within 15 mins.
6. Remove jars from water bath using jar lifters, cool it down within 12-24 hours before checking for proper sealing and storing.

Nutritional Values: Calories: 45; Carbs: 8g; Fat: 0g; Protein: 2g

43. Hamburger Dill Chips Pickles

Preparation time: 30 mins

Cooking time: 10 mins

Processing time: 10 mins

Yield: 6 pint jars

Ingredients:

- Eight cups sliced pickling cucumbers (about four pounds)
- Two cups white vinegar (5% acidity)
- Two cups water
- Four tablespoons granulated sugar
- One tablespoon pickling salt
- One tablespoon pickling spice mix
- Twelve fresh or dried dill sprigs (two sprigs per jar)

Directions:

1. Wash and slice the cucumbers into chips of about 1/4-inch thickness.
2. In your big pot, mix white vinegar, water, granulated sugar, pickling salt, plus pickling spice mix. Let it boil while mixing till sugar is dissolved. Adjust to a simmer within 5 mins.
3. Place two dill sprigs in each sterilized 6 pint jars. Divide the cucumber slices among the six jars with ½" headspace. Ladle hot brine over the cucumber slices with ½" headspace.
4. Remove any air bubbles using your bubble remover tool. Clean your jar rims, then secure with lids plus bands. Process jars in your water bath canner within 10 mins.
5. Remove jars from water bath using jar lifters, cool it down within 12-24 hours before checking for proper sealing and storing.

Nutritional Values: Calories: 11; Carbs: 1.9g; Fat: 0.1g; Protein: 0.4g

44. Southern Peaches Pickles

Preparation time: 20 mins

Cooking time: 10 mins

Processing time: 25 mins

Yield: 6 pint jars

Ingredients:

- Eight cups of fresh peaches, peeled, pitted, and sliced

- Two cups of granulated sugar
- One cup of light brown sugar, packed
- One and a half cups of apple cider vinegar
- One and a half teaspoons ground cinnamon
- Three-quarters teaspoon cloves, ground
- Half teaspoon ginger, ground
- Half teaspoon allspice, ground

Directions:

1. In your big stainless-steel saucepan, mix both sugars, apple cider vinegar, plus spices. Let it boil on moderate temp while mixing till sugar dissolved.
2. Add sliced peaches, then cook within 2 to 3 mins till heated through. Transfer cooked peaches into hot sterilized pint jars with ½" headspace.
3. Ladle remaining hot syrup over peaches. Remove any air bubbles using your bubble remover tool.
4. Clean your jar rims, then secure with lids plus bands. Process jars in your water bath canner within 25 mins.
5. Remove jars from water bath using jar lifters, cool it down within 12-24 hours before checking for proper sealing and storing.

Nutritional Values: Calories: 210; Carbs: 50g; Fat: 0g; Protein: 1g

45. Mustard Turmeric Pickles

Preparation time: 20 mins

Cooking time: 20 mins

Processing time: 10 mins

Yield: 6 pint jars

Ingredients:

- Six cups sliced cucumbers (approximately six to eight medium-sized cucumbers)
- One and a half cups thinly sliced onions
- Two cups white vinegar
- One and a half cups granulated sugar
- One and a half teaspoons ground turmeric
- One teaspoon mustard seeds, crushed
- One quarter teaspoon whole cloves
- One quarter teaspoon red pepper flakes (optional)

Directions:

1. Mix sliced cucumbers plus onions in your big container.
2. In your non-reactive saucepan, mix white vinegar, sugar, turmeric, mustard seeds, whole cloves, plus red pepper flakes (if using). Let it gently boil on moderate-high temp while mixing often.
3. Pour hot mixture over cucumbers and onions, ensuring all slices are fully coated. Stir well and let stand within 10 mins.
4. Using a slotted spoon or fork, carefully pack cucumber and onion slices into each jar leaving half an inch of space at the top.
5. Pour the remaining liquid into each jar over the top of the cucumber mixture to cover completely.
6. Remove any air bubbles with a non-metallic spatula by gently pressing against the sides of each jar.
7. Clean your jar rims, then secure with lids plus bands. Process jars in your water bath canner within 10 mins.
8. Remove jars from water bath using jar lifters, cool it down within 12-24 hours before checking for proper sealing and storing.

Nutritional Values: Calories: 30; Carbs: 7g; Fat: 0g; Protein: 0g

46. Garlic Dill Pickles

Preparation time: 20 mins

Cooking time: 5 mins

Processing time: 15 mins

Yield: About 7 pint jars

Ingredients:

- Four pounds of fresh pickling cucumbers, trimmed
- Twelve cups of water
- Four cups of white vinegar
- Two-thirds cup of pickling salt
- Fourteen cloves of garlic, peeled & halved
- Seven heads of dill weed, fresh
- Three-and-a-half teaspoons of red pepper flakes (optional)

Directions:

1. In your big pot, mix water, vinegar, plus pickling salt. Let it boil, stirring occasionally till salt dissolves.
2. In each pint jar, place two halved garlic cloves, one head of dill weed, and half a teaspoon of red pepper flakes (if desired).
3. Pack cucumbers into each with ½" headspace. Pour hot brine over cucumbers, maintaining that half-inch headspace.
4. Clean your jar rims, then secure with lids plus bands. Process jars in your water bath canner within 15 mins.

5. Remove jars from water bath using jar lifters, cool it down within 12-24 hours before checking for proper sealing and storing.

Nutritional Values: Calories: 50; Carbs: 12g; Fat: 0g; Protein: 1g

47. Spiced Berries with Bay Pickles

Preparation time: 20 mins

Cooking time: 10 mins

Processing time: 15 mins

Yield: 6 pint jars

Ingredients:

- Four pounds mixed berries (strawberries, blueberries, raspberries)
- Twelve whole bay leaves
- One and a half cups apple cider vinegar
- One and a half cups water
- Three cups granulated sugar
- One tablespoon whole black peppercorns
- One teaspoon whole allspice berries
- Half teaspoon ground cinnamon

Directions:

1. In your nonreactive saucepan, mix apple cider vinegar, water, sugar, black peppercorns, allspice berries, plus ground cinnamon. Let it boil on moderate temp while mixing well.
2. Place two bay leaves into 6 sterilized jars. Fill each jar halfway with the mixed berries.
3. Ladle hot pickling liquid over berries with ½" headspace. Remove any air bubbles using your bubble remover tool.
4. Clean your jar rims, then secure with lids plus bands. Process jars in your water bath canner within 15 mins.
5. Remove jars from water bath using jar lifters, cool it down within 12-24 hours before checking for proper sealing and storing.

Nutritional Values: Calories: 180; Carbs: 45g; Fat: 0g; Protein: 1g

48. Celery Seed Pickled Asparagus

Preparation time: 20 mins

Cooking time: 10 mins

Processing time: 10 mins

Yield: 4 pint jars

Ingredients:

- Two pounds fresh asparagus, trimmed
- Two cups apple cider vinegar
- Two cups water
- One-fourth cup granulated sugar
- Two tablespoons pickling salt
- One teaspoon celery seeds
- One teaspoon whole black peppercorns
- Four cloves garlic, peeled and halved

Directions:

1. In your big saucepan, mix apple cider vinegar, water, sugar, pickling salt, celery seeds, plus whole black peppercorns. Let it boil on moderate-high temp, stirring occasionally.
2. Divide garlic pieces between your sterilized jars. Pack asparagus spears vertically into jars as tightly as possible without crushing them.
3. Pour boiling brine over the asparagus spears in each jar leaving half an inch of headspace. Remove any air bubbles using your bubble remover tool.
4. Clean your jar rims, then secure with lids plus bands. Process jars in your water bath canner within 10 mins.
5. Remove jars from water bath using jar lifters, cool it down within 12-24 hours before checking for proper sealing and storing.

Nutritional Values: Calories: 172; Carbs: 25g; Fat: 4g; Protein: 6g

49. Jalapeño Pickles

Preparation time: 20 mins

Cooking time: 10 mins

Processing time: 5 mins

Yield: 8 pint jars

Ingredients:

- Twenty-five whole jalapeño peppers, sliced small slit in each
- Four cups white vinegar
- Four cups granulated sugar
- One tablespoon mustard seeds
- One teaspoon celery seeds
- Half teaspoon turmeric

Directions:

1. In your big saucepan, mix vinegar, sugar, mustard seeds, celery seeds, plus turmeric on moderate-high temp till sugar dissolves.
2. Fill your 8 sterilized jars with jalapeños, allowing a half-inch headspace. Carefully pour hot brine over jalapeños, leaving a quarter-inch headspace in each.
3. Remove any air bubbles using your bubble remover tool. Clean your jar rims, then secure with lids plus bands. Process jars in your water bath canner within 5 mins.
4. Remove jars from water bath using jar lifters, cool it down within 12-24 hours before checking for proper sealing and storing.

Nutritional Values: Calories: 49; Carbs: 12g; Fat: 0g; Protein: <1g

50. Sweet Watermelon Pickles

Preparation time: 30 mins

Cooking time: 1 hour

Processing time: 10 mins

Yield: 6 pint jars

Ingredients:

- Four cups of cubed watermelon rind, green skin removed
- Two cups of white sugar
- One and a half cups of distilled white vinegar
- Five whole cloves
- One tablespoon of whole black peppercorns
- One tablespoon of ground cinnamon
- One teaspoon of celery seeds

Directions:

1. In your big saucepan, mix sugar, vinegar, cloves, peppercorns, cinnamon, plus celery seeds. Let it boil while mixing till sugar dissolves.

2. Add watermelon rind cubes to the saucepan and adjust to a simmer. Cook rinds within 45 mins or until they become translucent. Remove saucepan, then cool it down within 10 mins.
3. Fill jars with watermelon pickles within half an inch of the rim. Pour the syrup over the pickles in each jar, leaving about quarter-inch headspace.
4. Remove any air bubbles using your bubble remover tool. Clean your jar rims, then secure with lids plus bands. Process jars in your water bath canner within 10 mins.
5. Remove jars from water bath using jar lifters, cool it down within 12-24 hours before checking for proper sealing and storing.

Nutritional Values: Calories: 124; Carbs: 31g; Fat: 0g; Protein: 0g

51. Classic Bread & Butter Pickles

Preparation time: 45 mins

Cooking time: 15 mins

Processing time: 10 mins

Yield: 6 pint jars

Ingredients:

- Eight cups sliced thinly cucumbers
- Two cups sliced thinly onions
- One-quarter cup kosher salt
- Four cups white vinegar
- Two and a half cups granulated sugar
- Two tablespoons mustard seeds
- One teaspoon celery seeds
- One teaspoon turmeric, ground

Directions:

1. In your big non-metallic bowl, mix cucumber slices, onion slices, plus kosher salt. Cover with enough cold water, then let it sit within 2 hours in your refrigerator.
2. Drain cucumber mixture, then wash thoroughly under cold water to remove excess salt.
3. In your big pot, mix white vinegar, granulated sugar, mustard & celery seeds, plus ground turmeric. Let it boil on moderate-high temp.
4. Add drained cucumber mixture, then let it boil again within 1 min. Ladle mixture into your sterilized jars with ½" headspace.
5. Remove any air bubbles using your bubble remover tool. Clean your jar rims, then secure with lids plus bands. Process jars in your water bath canner within 10 mins.
6. Remove jars from water bath using jar lifters, cool it down within 12-24 hours before checking for proper sealing and storing.

Nutritional Values: Calories: 72; Carbs: 16g; Fat: 0.2g; Protein: 0.7g

52. Basil Garlic Pickled Beans

Preparation time: 20 mins

Cooking time: 10 mins

Processing time: 15 mins

Yield: 6 pint jars

Ingredients:

- One and a half pounds fresh green beans, trimmed & sliced
- Six garlic cloves, peeled and sliced
- Six cups white vinegar (five percent acidity)
- Six cups filtered water
- One tablespoon coarse salt
- One tablespoon granulated sugar
- Twelve sprigs of fresh basil

Directions:

1. In your big saucepan, mix white vinegar, filtered water, salt, plus granulated sugar. Let it to boil on moderate-high temp while mixing.
2. Place one garlic clove and two sprigs of basil into each of the six sterilized pint jars. Divide the cut green beans among the jars, packing them tightly.
3. Carefully pour the hot vinegar mixture over the beans in each jar with ½" headspace. Remove any air bubbles using your bubble remover tool.
4. Clean your jar rims, then secure with lids plus bands. Process jars in your water bath canner within 15 mins.
5. Remove jars from water bath using jar lifters, cool it down within 12-24 hours before checking for proper sealing and storing.

Nutritional Values: Calories: 42; Carbs: 8g; Fat: 0g; Protein: 2g

53. Classic Pickled Cherries

Preparation time: 20 mins

Cooking time: 10 mins

Processing time: 15 mins

Yield: 6 pint jars

Ingredients:

- Four pounds of fresh sweet cherries, pitted
- Two cups of granulated sugar
- Two cups of apple cider vinegar
- One cup of water
- One tablespoon whole black peppercorns
- One teaspoon whole allspice berries
- Half a teaspoon of ground cinnamon
- Six cinnamon sticks, for garnish

Directions:

1. In your big saucepan, mix sugar, apple cider vinegar, water, black peppercorns, allspice berries, and ground cinnamon. Let it boil on moderate-high temp while mixing.
2. Carefully add pitted cherries to the boiling mixture. Stir gently and cook within 5 mins till cherries are heated.
3. Using a slotted spoon, pack the cherries and spices evenly into the prepared jars, leaving a half-inch headspace.
4. Pour the hot pickling liquid over the cherries in each jar with ½" headspace. Add one cinnamon stick into each jar. Remove any air bubbles using your bubble remover tool.
5. Clean your jar rims, then secure with lids plus bands. Process jars in your water bath canner within 15 mins.
6. Remove jars from water bath using jar lifters, cool it down within 12-24 hours before checking for proper sealing and storing.

Nutritional Values: Calories: 63; Carbs: 14g; Fat: 0g; Protein: 0.3g

54. Canned Mustard Pickles

Preparation time: 30 mins

Cooking time: 10 mins

Processing time: 15 mins

Yield: 6 pint jars

Ingredients:

- Four cups sliced cucumbers
- Two cups chopped onions
- Two cups chopped red bell pepper
- Two and a half tablespoons pickling salt
- One cup water
- Three cups white vinegar
- One cup sugar, granulated
- Quarter cup dry mustard powder
- Two tablespoons mustard seeds

Directions:

1. In your big non-reactive mixing bowl, mix sliced cucumbers, onions, plus red bell pepper. Add pickling salt and toss the vegetables lightly to coat evenly.
2. Add enough ice cubes to cover, then refrigerate within 4 hours. Drain vegetables, then gently wash under cold water to remove salt. Drain again.
3. In your big non-reactive saucepan, mix water, white vinegar, granulated sugar, dry mustard powder, plus mustard seeds. Cook on moderate temp while mixing often till sugar is dissolved.
4. Add drained vegetables to the saucepan, then boil it gently. Adjust to a simmer within 10 mins till vegetables are softened.

5. Pack mustard pickles into your sterilized jars with ½" headspace. Top with hot vinegar mixture to cover the vegetables. Remove any air bubbles using your bubble remover tool.
6. Clean your jar rims, then secure with lids plus bands. Process jars in your water bath canner within 15 mins.
7. Remove jars from water bath using jar lifters, cool it down within 12-24 hours before checking for proper sealing and storing.

Nutritional Values: Calories: 80; Carbs: 16g; Fat: 1g; Protein: 2g

55. Savory Garlic Pickles

Preparation time: 30 mins

Cooking time: 10 mins

Processing time: 15 mins

Yield: 6 pint jars

Ingredients:

- Four pounds pickling cucumbers
- Eight cups apple cider vinegar
- Two cups water
- Two tablespoons kosher salt
- Six tablespoons sugar
- Twelve garlic cloves, peeled and halved (fresh)
- Three teaspoons dill seed (whole)
- Six teaspoons yellow mustard seed (whole)
- Three teaspoons crushed red pepper flakes

Directions:

1. Wash and trim the cucumbers, then cut into spears or round slices. Set aside.
2. In your big non-reactive pot, mix apple cider vinegar, water, kosher salt, plus sugar. Let it boil.
3. Add two garlic cloves (half each) on the bottom of each jar. Distribute dill seed, yellow mustard seed, plus pepper flakes evenly between your jars.
4. Pack cucumbers tightly into each jar on top of the garlic and spices. Carefully pour hot brine in each jar with ½" headspace.
5. Remove any air bubbles using your bubble remover tool. Clean your jar rims, then secure with lids plus bands. Process jars in your water bath canner within 15 mins.
6. Remove jars from water bath using jar lifters, cool it down within 12-24 hours before checking for proper sealing and storing.

Nutritional Values: Calories: 53; Carbs: 8g; Fat: 0g; Protein: 1g

56. Classic Squash Pickles

Preparation time: 30 mins

Cooking time: 15 mins

Processing time: 10 mins

Yield: 6 pint jars

Ingredients:

- Four pounds yellow squash, thinly sliced
- Two medium onions, thinly sliced
- One and a half tablespoons salt
- Two cups granulated sugar
- Two cups white vinegar
- One cup water
- One teaspoon mustard seeds
- One teaspoon celery seeds
- Half a teaspoon ground turmeric

Directions:

1. In your big nonreactive container, mix squash plus onions. Flavor with salt, mix well, then let it sit within one hour. Drain.
2. Mix sugar, vinegar, water, mustard & celery seeds, plus turmeric in your big pot. Let it boil on moderate-high temp.
3. Add squash plus onions, mix well, then let it boil gently within 5 mins. Spoon mixture into your sterilized pint jars with ½" headspace. Ladle pickling liquid in each jar, maintaining ½" headspace.
4. Remove any air bubbles using your bubble remover tool. Clean your jar rims, then secure with lids plus bands. Process jars in your water bath canner within 10 mins.
5. Remove jars from water bath using jar lifters, cool it down within 12-24 hours before checking for proper sealing and storing.

Nutritional Values: Calories: 30; Carbs: 7g; Fat: 0g; Protein: 0g

57. Homemade Beet Pickles

Preparation time: 30 mins

Cooking time: 10 mins

Processing time: 30 mins

Yield: 8 pint jars

Ingredients:

- Twenty-five small to medium beets, trimmed
- Four cups white vinegar
- Two cups water
- Two cups granulated sugar
- One and a half teaspoons pickling salt
- One teaspoon whole allspice
- One teaspoon yellow mustard seeds

- Eight cloves garlic, peeled (one per jar)
- Eight sprigs fresh dill, washed (one per jar)

Directions:

1. Put beets in your big pot with enough water, then boil within 20 mins till tender. Drain, cool it down, peel them, then slice into chunks.
2. In your big saucepan, mix vinegar, water, sugar, pickling salt, whole allspice, plus mustard seeds. Let it boil on moderate-high temp till sugar is dissolved. Adjust to a simmer within 5 mins.
3. Place one garlic clove plus one dill sprig in each sterilized jar. Add beets in each with ½" headspace. Pour hot pickling liquid over beets, maintaining a ½" headspace.
4. Remove any air bubbles using your bubble remover tool. Clean your jar rims, then secure with lids plus bands. Process jars in your water bath canner within 30 mins.
5. Remove jars from water bath using jar lifters, cool it down within 12-24 hours before checking for proper sealing and storing.

Nutritional Values: Calories: 50; Carbs: 12g; Fat: 0g; Protein: 1g

58. Baby Carrots Pickles

Preparation time: 30 mins

Cooking time: 10 mins

Processing time: 10 mins

Yield: 6 pint jars

Ingredients:

- Two pounds of fresh baby carrots
- Three cups of distilled white vinegar
- Two cups of water
- One cup of granulated sugar
- Two tablespoons of pickling salt
- One tablespoon of yellow mustard seeds
- One teaspoon of dill seeds
- Six whole cloves of garlic, peeled
- Six sprigs of fresh dill

Directions:

1. Begin by washing and peeling the baby carrots, trimming off any green tops if necessary.
2. In your big saucepan, mix distilled white vinegar, water, granulated sugar, plus pickling salt. Let it boil on moderate-high temp. Adjust to low temp, then simmer within 10 mins.
3. Place one clove of garlic, one sprig of dill, half a tablespoon of yellow mustard seeds, and one-sixth a teaspoon of dill seeds into each jar.
4. Pack the baby carrots into each jar vertically so they are evenly distributed.
5. Ladle the vinegar mixture over the baby carrots in each jar, ensuring they are fully covered with ½" headspace.

6. Remove any air bubbles using your bubble remover tool. Clean your jar rims, then secure with lids plus bands. Process jars in your water bath canner within 10 mins.
7. Remove jars from water bath using jar lifters, cool it down within 12-24 hours before checking for proper sealing and storing.

Nutritional Values: Calories: 45; Carbs: 9g; Fat: 0.5g; Protein: 0.5g

59. Spicy Onions Pickle

Preparation time: 20 mins

Cooking time: 5 mins

Processing time: 15 mins

Yield: 6 pint jars

Ingredients:

- Four pounds of yellow onions, thinly sliced
- Two cups apple cider vinegar
- Two cups water
- One cup granulated sugar
- One tablespoon pickling salt
- One tablespoon red pepper flakes, crushed
- Six cloves of garlic, peeled and halved

Directions:

1. In your big saucepan, mix vinegar, water, sugar, pickling salt, plus crushed red pepper flakes. Let it boil on moderate temp while mixing till sugar dissolves.
2. Add onion slices plus garlic halves, then cook within 5 mins till onions have slightly softened.
3. Evenly distribute onion slices plus garlic into sterilized pint jars. Carefully ladle the hot pickling liquid into each jar with ½" headspace.
4. Remove any air bubbles using your bubble remover tool. Clean your jar rims, then secure with lids plus bands. Process jars in your water bath canner within 15 mins.
5. Remove jars from water bath using jar lifters, cool it down within 12-24 hours before checking for proper sealing and storing.

Nutritional Values: Calories: 80; Carbs: 18g; Fat: 0g; Protein: 1g

60. Red Cabbage Pickle

Preparation time: 20 mins

Cooking time: 10 mins

Processing time: 15 mins

Yield: 6 pint jars

Ingredients:

- One medium-sized red cabbage, finely shredded
- Two and a half cups of apple cider vinegar
- One cup of water
- One and a half cups of granulated sugar
- Four teaspoons of pickling salt
- Three teaspoons of caraway seeds

Directions:

1. Mix apple cider vinegar, water, granulated sugar, plus pickling salt in your pot. Let it boil on moderate-high temp.
2. Mix in shredded red cabbage plus caraway seeds. Adjust to moderate-low temp, then simmer within 5 mins till cabbage begins to soften.
3. Fill sterilized pint jars with cooked cabbage with ¼" headspace. Pour hot vinegar mixture over cabbage, maintaining the ¼" headspace.
4. Remove any air bubbles using your bubble remover tool. Clean your jar rims, then secure with lids plus bands. Process jars in your water bath canner within 15 mins.
5. Remove jars from water bath using jar lifters, cool it down within 12-24 hours before checking for proper sealing and storing.

Nutritional Values: Calories 100; Carbs 25g; Fat 0g; Protein 1g

Chapter 12. RELISH & CHUTNEY

61. Zucchini Pepper Relish

Preparation time: 30 mins

Cooking time: 20 mins

Processing time: 15 mins

Yield: 8 cups

Ingredients:

- Four medium-sized zucchinis, finely diced
- Two red bell peppers, finely diced
- Two green bell peppers, finely diced
- One large onion, finely chopped
- Two cups apple cider vinegar
- One and a half cups granulated sugar
- Half cup diced sweet pickles
- One tablespoon salt
- One teaspoon celery seed
- Half teaspoon ground mustard
- Quarter teaspoon ground turmeric
- Quarter teaspoon black pepper

Directions:

1. In your big container, mix zucchinis, bell peppers, plus onion.
2. In your non-reactive saucepan, mix apple cider vinegar, sugar, sweet pickles, salt, celery seed, ground mustard, ground turmeric, plus black pepper. Let it boil on moderate temp.
3. Add zucchini-pepper mixture, then let it boil. Adjust to a simmer within 10 mins till vegetables are tender.
4. Carefully ladle hot relish into your sterilized jars with ½" headspace. Remove any air bubbles using your bubble remover tool.
5. Clean your jar rims, then secure with lids plus bands. Process jars in your water bath canner within 15 mins.
6. Remove jars from water bath using jar lifters, cool it down within 12-24 hours before checking for proper sealing and storing.

Nutritional Values: Calories: 25; Carbs: 5g; Fat: 0g; Protein: 0.3g

62. Jalapeno Pepper Relish

Preparation time: 20 mins

Cooking time: 10 mins

Processing time: 15 mins

Yield: 6 half-pint jars

Ingredients:

- One cup finely chopped onions
- Three cups chopped each green & red bell peppers
- One and a half cups finely chopped jalapeno peppers
- Two, one-fourth cups white vinegar
- Three-quarters cup granulated sugar
- One tablespoon salt

Directions:

1. Mix onions, bell peppers, plus jalapeno peppers in your big container.
2. In your medium saucepan, mix white vinegar, granulated sugar, plus salt. Let it boil on moderate temp while mixing.
3. Add pepper mixture, then let it boil. Adjust to a simmer within 10 mins, mixing often. Remove, then cool it down slightly.
4. Ladle mixture into your sterilized half-pint jars with ½" headspace. Remove any air bubbles using your bubble remover tool.
5. Clean your jar rims, then secure with lids plus bands. Process jars in your water bath canner within 15 mins.
6. Remove jars from water bath using jar lifters, cool it down within 12-24 hours before checking for proper sealing and storing.

Nutritional Values: Calories: 60; Carbs: 12g; Fat: 0g; Protein: 1g

63. Classic Cranberry Relish

Preparation time: 20 mins

Cooking time: 15 mins

Processing time: 10 mins

Yield: 6 cups

Ingredients:

- Four cups cranberries
- Two cups sugar
- One cup water
- One small orange, zested and juiced
- One small lemon, zested and juiced
- One teaspoon cinnamon, ground
- Half teaspoon cloves, ground

Directions:

1. Mix cranberries, sugar, plus water in your big saucepan on moderate temp.
2. Add orange zest, orange juice, lemon zest, lemon juice, cinnamon, plus cloves to the saucepan. Cook within 10-12 mins till cranberries burst. Remove, then cool it down slightly.
3. Ladle mixture into your sterilized half-pint jars with ½" headspace. Remove any air bubbles using your bubble remover tool.
4. Clean your jar rims, then secure with lids plus bands. Process jars in your water bath canner within 10 mins.
5. Remove jars from water bath using jar lifters, cool it down within 12-24 hours before checking for proper sealing and storing.

Nutritional Values: Calories: 45; Carbs: 11g; Fat: 0g; Protein: 0g

64. Sweet Pepper Pickle Relish

Preparation time: 1 hour

Cooking time: 20 mins

Processing time: 15 mins

Yield: 8 half-pint jars

Ingredients:

- Four cups chopped each green & red bell pepper
- One & half cups finely chopped onion
- One & half teaspoons salt
- Two cups apple cider vinegar
- Two cups white sugar
- One teaspoon whole mustard seeds
- One teaspoon celery seeds

Directions:

1. In your big non-reactive container, mix bell peppers, plus onion. Add salt and mix well. Let it sit within 1 hour. Drain.
2. In your big heavy-bottomed pot on moderate temp, mix vinegar, sugar, mustard seeds, plus celery seeds.
3. Add drained vegetable mixture, let it boil, then adjust to low temp. Simmer within 20 mins, mixing often.

4. Ladle mixture into your sterilized half-pint jars with ½" headspace. Remove any air bubbles using your bubble remover tool.
5. Clean your jar rims, then secure with lids plus bands. Process jars in your water bath canner within 15 mins.
6. Remove jars from water bath using jar lifters, cool it down within 12-24 hours before checking for proper sealing and storing.

Nutritional Values: Calories: 54; Carbs: 13g; Fat: 0g; Protein: 0.5g

65. Tomato Olive Relish

Preparation time: 15 mins

Cooking time: 10 mins

Processing time: 15 mins

Yield: 4 half-pint jars

Ingredients:

- Two cups of diced ripe tomatoes
- One cup of pitted and chopped green olives
- One cup of pitted and chopped black olives
- Half a cup of finely chopped red onion
- One third of a cup of cider vinegar
- One fourth of a cup of granulated sugar
- Two cloves of minced garlic
- Half a teaspoon of dried basil
- Half a teaspoon of dried oregano
- Quarter teaspoon of black pepper

Directions:

1. In your big saucepan, mix diced tomatoes, olives, red onion, cider vinegar, sugar, garlic, dried basil, dried oregano, and black pepper.
2. Let it boil on moderate temp, then simmer within 10 mins till mixture slightly thickens.
3. Ladle mixture into your sterilized half-pint jars with ½" headspace. Remove any air bubbles using your bubble remover tool.
4. Clean your jar rims, then secure with lids plus bands. Process jars in your water bath canner within 15 mins.

5. Remove jars from water bath using jar lifters, cool it down within 12-24 hours before checking for proper sealing and storing.

Nutritional Values: Calories: 25; Carbs: 3g; Fat: 1g; Protein: 0g

66. Green Tomato Relish

Preparation time: 30 mins

Cooking time: 1 hour

Processing time: 15 mins

Yield: 6 pint jars

Ingredients:

- Four pounds of green tomatoes, coarsely chopped
- One large sweet onion, finely chopped
- Two cups of green bell pepper, finely chopped
- Two cups of red bell pepper, finely chopped
- Four cloves of garlic, minced
- One cup of pure apple cider vinegar
- One and a half cups of granulated sugar
- One tablespoon of kosher salt
- One tablespoon of celery seed
- One teaspoon of yellow mustard seed

Directions:

1. Mix all fixings your big non-reactive pot, then let it boil on moderate-high temp. Adjust to a simmer within one hour till thickened, mixing often.
2. Ladle mixture into your sterilized half-pint jars with 1/4" headspace. Remove any air bubbles using your bubble remover tool.
3. Clean your jar rims, then secure with lids plus bands. Process jars in your water bath canner within 15 mins.
4. Remove jars from water bath using jar lifters, cool it down within 12-24 hours before checking for proper sealing and storing.

Nutritional Values: Calories: 13; Carbs: 2.9g; Fat: 0.1g; Protein: 0.2g

67. Tangy Beet Relish

Preparation time: 30 mins

Cooking time: 20 mins

Processing time: 30 mins

Yield: 6 eight-ounce jars

Ingredients:

- Seven cups grated beets, unpeeled (approximately eight medium beets)
- One and a half cups finely chopped onion
- One and a quarter cups finely chopped green bell pepper
- Two cups granulated sugar
- One teaspoon salt
- Two teaspoons whole cloves
- Two cinnamon sticks, broken in half
- Three cups apple cider vinegar

Directions:

1. In your big stainless steel saucepan on moderate temp, mix granulated sugar, salt, whole cloves, cinnamon sticks, and apple cider vinegar.
2. Add grated beets, onion, plus bell pepper. Let it boil on moderate temp, adjust to low temp, then simmer within 20 mins, mixing often.
3. Remove cinnamon sticks plus whole cloves from the mixture using a slotted spoon; discard them.
4. Using a ladle or spoon, fill the sterilized jars with relish with ½" headspace. Remove any air bubbles using your bubble remover tool.
5. Clean your jar rims, then secure with lids plus bands. Process jars in your water bath canner within 30 mins.
6. Remove jars from water bath using jar lifters, cool it down within 12-24 hours before checking for proper sealing and storing.

Nutritional Values: Calories: 21; Carbs: 4g; Fat: 0g; Protein: 0g

68. Cranberry Raspberry Relish

Preparation time: 20 mins

Cooking time: 15 mins

Processing time: 10 mins

Yield: 6 cups

Ingredients:

- Four cups fresh cranberries
- Two cups fresh raspberries
- One & half cups granulated sugar
- One cup orange juice
- One tablespoon orange zest
- Half a teaspoon cinnamon, ground
- Quarter teaspoon nutmeg, ground

Directions:

1. In your big saucepan, mix cranberries, raspberries, sugar, orange juice, zest, cinnamon, plus nutmeg.
2. Cook on moderate temp, mixing often till cranberries start to pop. Adjust to low temp, then simmer within 10 mins till relish thickens. Remove, then cool it down.
3. Ladle mixture into your sterilized half-pint jars with 1/4" headspace. Remove any air bubbles using your bubble remover tool.
4. Clean your jar rims, then secure with lids plus bands. Process jars in your water bath canner within 10 mins.
5. Remove jars from water bath using jar lifters, cool it down within 12-24 hours before checking for proper sealing and storing.

Nutritional Values: Calories: 225; Carbs: 55g; Fat: 0g; Protein: 1g

69. Spiced Apple Relish

Preparation time: 20 mins

Cooking time: 25 mins

Processing time: 10 mins

Yield: 6 half-pint jars

Ingredients:

- Two cups peeled, cored, & diced apples
- One cup chopped onion
- One cup chopped red bell pepper
- Half cup apple cider vinegar
- Half cup granulated sugar
- One tablespoon cinnamon, ground
- One teaspoon ginger, ground
- One teaspoon mustard seed, ground
- Half teaspoon cloves, ground
- Quarter teaspoon crushed red pepper flakes

Directions:

1. In your big saucepan, mix apples, onion, red bell pepper, apple cider vinegar, sugar, cinnamon, ginger, mustard seed, cloves, plus red pepper flakes.
2. Let it boil on moderate-high temp, adjust to low temp, then simmer within 25 mins till apples are tender.
3. Ladle mixture into your sterilized jars with 1/4" headspace. Remove any air bubbles using your bubble remover tool.
4. Clean your jar rims, then secure with lids plus bands. Process jars in your water bath canner within 10 mins.
5. Remove jars from water bath using jar lifters, cool it down within 12-24 hours before checking for proper sealing and storing.

Nutritional Values: Calories: 13; Carbs: 3g; Fat: 0g; Protein: 0g

70. Sweet Rhubarb Chutney

Preparation time: 20 mins

Cooking time: 40 mins

Processing time: 15 mins

Yield: 6 cups

Ingredients:

- Four cups of finely chopped rhubarb
- One & half cups of granulated sugar
- One cup of apple cider vinegar
- Half cup raisins
- Half cup chopped onion
- Two cloves of minced garlic
- One tablespoon of freshly grated ginger root

- Half tablespoon cinnamon, ground
- Half tablespoon allspice, ground

Directions:

1. In your big stainless steel saucepan, mix rhubarb, sugar, vinegar, raisins, chopped onion, minced garlic, grated ginger root, ground cinnamon, and ground allspice.
2. Let it boil on moderate-high temp, mixing often. Adjust to a simmer within 30 mins till chutney has thickened, mixing often.
3. Ladle mixture into your sterilized jars with 1/4" headspace. Remove any air bubbles using your bubble remover tool.
4. Clean your jar rims, then secure with lids plus bands. Process jars in your water bath canner within 15 mins.
5. Remove jars from water bath using jar lifters, cool it down within 12-24 hours before checking for proper sealing and storing.

Nutritional Values: Calories: 97; Carbs: 24g; Fat: 0.2g; Protein: 0.8g

71. Spicy Mango Chutney

Preparation time: 30 mins

Cooking time: 40 mins

Processing time: 10 mins

Yield: Four 8-ounce jars

Ingredients:

- Four large ripe mangoes, peeled & diced
- One cup apple cider vinegar
- One & half cups granulated sugar
- One red bell pepper, deseeded and chopped
- Half cup golden raisins
- Half cup chopped red onion
- Two garlic cloves, minced
- One tablespoon fresh ginger, grated
- One teaspoon red pepper flakes (adjust according to desired heat)
- Half a teaspoon cinnamon, ground
- Quarter teaspoon cloves, ground

Directions:

1. In your big saucepan, mix diced mangoes, apple cider vinegar, plus sugar. Let it boil on moderate temp.

2. Add chopped red bell pepper, golden raisins, chopped red onion, minced garlic, grated ginger, red pepper flakes, cinnamon, plus ground cloves. Mix well.
3. Adjust to low temp, then simmer within 30 to 40 mins till chutney has thickened; mixing often.
4. Ladle mixture into your sterilized jars with 1/2" headspace. Remove any air bubbles using your bubble remover tool.
5. Clean your jar rims, then secure with lids plus bands. Process jars in your water bath canner within 15 mins.
6. Remove jars from water bath using jar lifters, cool it down within 12-24 hours before checking for proper sealing and storing.

Nutritional Values: Calories: 60; Carbs: 15g; Fat: 0g; Protein: 0.2g

72. Plum Tomato Chutney

Preparation time: 30 mins

Cooking time: 45 mins

Processing time: 20 mins

Yield: 6 half-pint jars

Ingredients:

- Three pounds of plum tomatoes, coarsely chopped
- One large yellow onion, finely chopped
- One clove of garlic, minced
- One cup of dark brown sugar,
- Half cup apple cider vinegar
- Half cup golden raisins
- One-fourth cup of fresh ginger, grated
- One teaspoon of yellow mustard seeds
- Half teaspoon each of ground cinnamon and allspice
- Half teaspoon each of ground nutmeg and cayenne pepper
- One teaspoon salt

Directions:

1. In your big, non-reactive saucepan, mix tomatoes, onion, garlic, brown sugar, apple cider vinegar, raisins, ginger, mustard seeds, cinnamon, allspice, nutmeg, cayenne pepper, plus salt. Let it boil on moderate temp.
2. Adjust to low temp, then simmer within 45 mins till thickened; mixing often.
3. Ladle mixture into your sterilized jars with 1/2" headspace. Remove any air bubbles using your bubble remover tool.

4. Clean your jar rims, then secure with lids plus bands. Process jars in your water bath canner within 20 mins.
5. Remove jars from water bath using jar lifters, cool it down within 12-24 hours before checking for proper sealing and storing.

Nutritional Values: Calories: 110; Carbs: 25g; Fat: 0.5g; Protein: 1g

73. Spiced Plum Chutney

Preparation time: 15 mins

Cooking time: 45 mins

Processing time: 10 mins

Yield: 4 to 5 half-pint jars

Ingredients:

- Two pounds of fresh plums, pitted and chopped
- One cup of light brown sugar
- One cup of white distilled vinegar
- One small red onion, finely chopped
- Half a cup of golden raisins
- One tablespoon of freshly grated ginger
- Two teaspoons mustard seeds
- Half a teaspoon cinnamon, ground
- Quarter teaspoon cloves, ground
- Half teaspoon salt

Directions:

1. In your big, non-reactive saucepan, mix all fixings on moderate temp till sugar dissolves.
2. Let it boil, adjust to low temp, then simmer within 45 mins till mixture thickens.
3. Ladle mixture into your sterilized jars with 1/2" headspace. Remove any air bubbles using your bubble remover tool.
4. Clean your jar rims, then secure with lids plus bands. Process jars in your water bath canner within 10 mins.
5. Remove jars from water bath using jar lifters, cool it down within 12-24 hours before checking for proper sealing and storing.

Nutritional Values: Calories: 130; Carbs: 32g; Fat: 0g; Protein: 1g

74. Raisin Pear Chutney

Preparation time: 20 mins

Cooking time: 45 mins

Processing time: 10 mins

Yield: 6 half-pint jars

Ingredients:

- Four cups chopped, cored, and peeled ripe pears
- One and a half cups raisins
- One cup finely chopped onion
- One cup brown sugar, packed
- One tablespoon mustard seeds
- Two teaspoons curry powder
- One teaspoon ground allspice
- Half teaspoon salt
- Two cups apple cider vinegar

Directions:

1. In your big stainless-steel saucepan, mix all fixings on moderate temp till boiling.
2. Adjust to a simmer gently, uncovered, within 45 mins till chutney thickens; mixing often. Stir occasionally during this process.
3. Ladle mixture into your sterilized jars with 1/4" headspace. Remove any air bubbles using your bubble remover tool.
4. Clean your jar rims, then secure with lids plus bands. Process jars in your water bath canner within 10 mins.
5. Remove jars from water bath using jar lifters, cool it down within 12-24 hours before checking for proper sealing and storing.

Nutritional Values: Calories: 190; Carbs: 44g; Fat: 1g; Protein: 2g

75. Jalapeno-Pear Chutney

Preparation time: 20 mins

Cooking time: 45 mins

Processing time: 10 mins

Yield: 6 half-pint jars

Ingredients:

- Four cups of firm, ripe pears, peeled, cored, & chopped
- One and a half cups of onions, chopped
- One cup of jalapeno peppers, seeded & chopped
- One cup of red bell pepper, chopped
- One cup of apple cider vinegar
- Three fourths cup of brown sugar
- Two tablespoons of fresh ginger, minced
- One and a half teaspoons of mustard seeds
- One teaspoon of salt

Directions:

1. Mix pears, onions, jalapeno peppers, red bell pepper, apple cider vinegar, brown sugar, ginger, mustard seeds, plus salt in your big stainless-steel saucepan.
2. Let it boil on moderate-high temp. Adjust to moderate-low temp, then simmer while mixing within 45 mins till it thickens slightly. Remove any foam on top.
3. Ladle mixture into your sterilized jars with 1/4" headspace. Remove any air bubbles using your bubble remover tool.
4. Clean your jar rims, then secure with lids plus bands. Process jars in your water bath canner within 10 mins.
5. Remove jars from water bath using jar lifters, cool it down within 12-24 hours before checking for proper sealing and storing.

Nutritional Values: Calories: 109; Carbs: 26g; Fat: 0.3g; Protein: 0.9g

Chapter 13. SALSAS & SAUCES

76. Mexican Fiesta Salsa

Preparation time: 45 mins

Cooking time: 15 mins

Processing time: 20 mins

Yield: 6 pint jars

Ingredients:

- Four cups chopped ripe tomatoes
- Two and a half cups chopped white onion
- One and a half cups chopped green bell pepper
- One and a half cups chopped red bell pepper
- Eight ounces jalapeno peppers, finely chopped (about ten peppers)
- Three cloves garlic, minced
- Two teaspoons salt
- Two teaspoons black pepper
- One teaspoon ground cumin
- One cup apple cider vinegar (5% acidity)
- Half cup chopped fresh cilantro

Directions:

1. Wash and chop all vegetables. Make sure to remove seeds and membranes from peppers if you want a milder salsa.
2. In your big stainless steel saucepan, mix tomatoes, onions, bell peppers, jalapenos, garlic, salt, black pepper, plus cumin.
3. Add vinegar to the vegetable mixture, then let it boil on moderate-high temp. Adjust to a simmer within 15 mins, mixing often. Stir in cilantro just before filling jars.
4. Ladle mixture into your sterilized jars with 1/2" headspace. Remove any air bubbles using your bubble remover tool.
5. Clean your jar rims, then secure with lids plus bands. Process jars in your water bath canner within 20 mins.
6. Remove jars from water bath using jar lifters, cool it down within 12-24 hours before checking for proper sealing and storing.

Nutritional Values: Calories 5; Carbs 1g; Fat 0g; Protein 0g

77. Mild Tomato Pepper Salsa

Preparation time: 30 mins

Cooking time: 20 mins

Processing time: 15 mins

Yield: 8 cups

Ingredients:

- Six cups chopped tomatoes
- Two cups chopped bell peppers (combination of green and red)
- One cup chopped onions
- Half a cup chopped, seeded jalapeños (approximately four)
- Four cloves minced garlic
- One-fourth cup tightly packed chopped cilantro
- One tablespoon salt
- Half a tablespoon black pepper
- Half a cup apple cider vinegar

Directions:

1. In your big stockpot, mix tomatoes, bell peppers, onions, jalapeños, garlic, cilantro, salt, black pepper, plus apple cider vinegar. Let it boil, then adjust to a simmer within 20 mins, mixing often.
2. Ladle mixture into your sterilized jars with 1/2" headspace. Remove any air bubbles using your bubble remover tool.
3. Clean your jar rims, then secure with lids plus bands. Process jars in your water bath canner within 15 mins.
4. Remove jars from water bath using jar lifters, cool it down within 12-24 hours before checking for proper sealing and storing.

Nutritional Values: Calories: 15; Carbs: 3g; Fat: 0g; Protein: 1g

78. Red Onion & Tomato Salsa

Preparation time: 20 mins

Cooking time: 10 mins

Processing time: 15 mins

Yield: 5 pint jars

Ingredients:

- Six cups diced ripe tomatoes
- Two cups finely chopped red onions
- One and a half cups chopped fresh cilantro

- Half a cup freshly squeezed lime juice
- Four tablespoons minced garlic
- Two teaspoons cumin, ground
- One teaspoon each salt & black pepper
- Half a teaspoon crushed red pepper flakes (adjust to taste)

Directions:

1. In your big stainless-steel saucepan, mix tomatoes, red onions, cilantro, lime juice, minced garlic, cumin, salt, pepper, plus pepper flakes.
2. Let it boil on moderate-high temp, mixing often. Adjust to a simmer uncovered within 10 mins.
3. Ladle mixture into your sterilized jars with 1/2" headspace. Remove any air bubbles using your bubble remover tool.
4. Clean your jar rims, then secure with lids plus bands. Process jars in your water bath canner within 15 mins.
5. Remove jars from water bath using jar lifters, cool it down within 12-24 hours before checking for proper sealing and storing.

Nutritional Values: Calories: 15; Carbs: 3g; Fat: 0g; Protein: 1g

79. Fresh Green Salsa

Preparation time: 20 mins

Cooking time: 10 mins

Processing time: 15 mins

Yield: 4 pint jars

Ingredients:

- Four cups finely chopped tomatillos
- One cup chopped each onion & green bell pepper
- Two tablespoons minced garlic
- Two jalapeños, finely chopped
- Half cup chopped fresh cilantro
- Half cup freshly squeezed lime juice
- Half teaspoon ground cumin
- One teaspoon sea salt

Directions:

1. Combine all ingredients in your big saucepan, then let it boil. Adjust to a simmer within 10 mins.
2. Ladle mixture into your sterilized jars with 1/2" headspace. Remove any air bubbles using your bubble remover tool.
3. Clean your jar rims, then secure with lids plus bands. Process jars in your water bath canner within 15 mins.
4. Remove jars from water bath using jar lifters, cool it down within 12-24 hours before checking for proper sealing and storing.

Nutritional Values: Calories: 40; Carbs: 8g; Fat: 0g; Protein: 1g

80. Unripe Tomato Salsa

Preparation time: 30 mins

Cooking time: 10 mins

Processing time: 15 mins

Yield: 6 pints

Ingredients:

- Eight cups unripe tomatoes, chopped
- Two cups green bell pepper, chopped
- One and a half cups red onion, finely chopped
- One cup jalapeno pepper, minced
- Half a cup fresh cilantro, chopped
- Half a cup lime juice
- Four cloves garlic, minced
- Two teaspoons cumin, ground
- One teaspoon salt
- Half a teaspoon black pepper

Directions:

1. In your big stainless steel saucepan, mix chopped unripe tomatoes, bell pepper, red onion, jalapeno pepper, lime juice, garlic, cilantro, ground cumin, salt, plus black pepper.
2. Let it boil on moderate-high temp, then mix often. Let it simmer within 10 mins.
3. Ladle mixture into your sterilized jars with 1/2" headspace. Remove any air bubbles using your bubble remover tool.
4. Clean your jar rims, then secure with lids plus bands. Process jars in your water bath canner within 15 mins.
5. Remove jars from water bath using jar lifters, cool it down within 12-24 hours before checking for proper sealing and storing.

Nutritional Values: Calories: 12; Carbs: 2g; Fat: 0g; Protein: 0.5g

81. Lemon Strawberry Sauce

Preparation time: 15 mins

Cooking time: 20 mins

Processing time: 10 mins

Yield: 6 cups

Ingredients:

- Four cups fresh strawberries, hulled and quartered
- One cup granulated sugar
- One tablespoon lemon zest, freshly grated
- Three tablespoons lemon juice, freshly squeezed
- Half a teaspoon vanilla extract

Directions:

1. In your big saucepan, mix strawberries and sugar. Let it sit within 5 mins to allow strawberries to release their juices.
2. Put your saucepan on moderate temp, then mix in zest, lemon juice, plus vanilla extract. Cook mixture, stirring occasionally until the sugar dissolves completely.
3. Let it boil gently, then stir frequently within 20 mins till mixture thickness. Remove saucepan, then let it cool slightly.
4. Ladle mixture into your sterilized jars with 1/4" headspace. Remove any air bubbles using your bubble remover tool.
5. Clean your jar rims, then secure with lids plus bands. Process jars in your water bath canner within 10 mins.
6. Remove jars from water bath using jar lifters, cool it down within 12-24 hours before checking for proper sealing and storing.

Nutritional Values: Calories: 60; Carbs: 15g; Fat: 0g; Protein: 0g

82. Summer Tomato Sauce

Preparation time: 30 mins

Cooking time: 45 mins

Processing time: 40 mins

Yield: 6 pint jars

Ingredients:

- Eight pounds of fresh tomatoes, coarsely chopped
- Two medium onions, thinly sliced
- Four cloves of garlic, minced
- One cup of chopped fresh basil
- Two teaspoons of chopped fresh oregano
- Two teaspoons of salt
- One teaspoon of ground black pepper

- Half a cup of lemon juice, freshly squeezed

Directions:

1. In your big pot, mix tomatoes, onions, garlic, basil, oregano, salt, plus pepper. Simmer within 45 mins on low temp, mixing often. Mix in lemon juice.
2. Ladle mixture into your sterilized jars with 1/2" headspace. Remove any air bubbles using your bubble remover tool.
3. Clean your jar rims, then secure with lids plus bands. Process jars in your water bath canner within 40 mins.
4. Remove jars from water bath using jar lifters, cool it down within 12-24 hours before checking for proper sealing and storing.

Nutritional Values: Calories: 61; Carbs: 13g; Fat: 0.5g; Protein: 2g

83. Classic Pizza Sauce

Preparation time: 20 mins

Cooking time: 35 mins

Processing time: 40 mins

Yield: 8 cups

Ingredients:

- Eight cups fresh tomatoes, finely chopped
- One cup chopped onion
- Four cloves garlic, minced
- One tablespoon olive oil
- One tablespoon dried basil
- One tablespoon dried oregano
- One teaspoon salt
- Half a teaspoon black pepper
- Five tablespoons bottled lemon juice

Directions:

1. In your big stockpot, warm up olive oil on moderate temp. Add onions plus garlic, then sauté within 5 mins till soft.
2. Add tomatoes, basil, oregano, salt, plus black pepper. Let it boil, adjust to low temp, then simmer uncovered within 30 mins, mixing often till thickens. Mix in lemon juice.
3. Once the sauce has thickened to desired consistency, remove it from heat. Stir in the bottled lemon juice.
4. Ladle mixture into your sterilized jars with 1/2" headspace. Remove any air bubbles using your bubble remover tool.
5. Clean your jar rims, then secure with lids plus bands. Process jars in your water bath canner within 40 mins.
6. Remove jars from water bath using jar lifters, cool it down within 12-24 hours before checking for proper sealing and storing.

Nutritional Values: Calories: 21; Carbs: 3g; Fat: 1g; Protein: 0.7g

84. Pear Barbecue Sauce

Preparation time: 20 mins

Cooking time: 40 mins

Processing time: 15 mins

Yield: 6 half-pint jars

Ingredients:

- Four cups peeled, cored, & chopped ripe pears
- One cup onion, chopped
- Two cloves minced garlic
- One tablespoon olive oil
- Two cups ketchup
- Half a cup apple cider vinegar
- Half a cup brown sugar, packed
- One teaspoon mustard, ground
- Half teaspoon ginger, ground
- Half teaspoon cinnamon, ground
- Half teaspoon black pepper, ground
- Half teaspoon salt

Directions:

1. In your big saucepan, warm up olive oil on moderate temp. Add onion plus garlic, then cook within 5 mins till softened. Mix in chopped pears, then cook within 5 mins till soften.
2. Add ketchup, apple cider, brown sugar, ground mustard, ground ginger, ground cinnamon, ground black pepper, and salt to the saucepan.
3. Let it simmer on moderate-low temp, then cook within 30 mins, mixing often. Carefully blend sauce in your blender till smooth.
4. Ladle mixture into your sterilized jars with 1/4" headspace. Remove any air bubbles using your bubble remover tool.
5. Clean your jar rims, then secure with lids plus bands. Process jars in your water bath canner within 15 mins.
6. Remove jars from water bath using jar lifters, cool it down within 12-24 hours before checking for proper sealing and storing.

Nutritional Values: Calories: 194; Carbs: 47g; Fat: 1g; Protein: 1g

85. Basil-Garlic Tomato Sauce

Preparation time: 30 mins

Cooking time: 40 mins

Processing time: 35 mins

Yield: 8 cups

Ingredients:

- Eight pounds ripe tomatoes, chopped
- One large chopped onion
- Four cloves minced garlic
- One-fourth cup fresh basil, chopped
- One teaspoon salt
- Half teaspoon black pepper, ground
- Half teaspoon sugar

Directions:

1. In your big pot, mix chopped tomatoes, onions, plus garlic. Let it boil on moderate temp, then cook within 20 mins till tomatoes are soft. Blend cooked tomato mixture in your blender till smooth.
2. Add tomato mixture, chopped basil, salt, pepper, plus sugar to your pot. Stir well to combine and simmer for another 20 mins.
3. Ladle mixture into your sterilized jars with 1/4" headspace. Remove any air bubbles using your bubble remover tool.
4. Clean your jar rims, then secure with lids plus bands. Process jars in your water bath canner within 35 mins.
5. Remove jars from water bath using jar lifters, cool it down within 12-24 hours before checking for proper sealing and storing.

Nutritional Values: Calories 110; Carbs 24g; Fat 1g; Protein 5g

PRESSURE CANNING RECIPES

Chapter 14.   VEGETABLES

86. Hearty Veggie Chili

Preparation time: 30 mins

Cooking time: 15 mins

Processing time: 90 mins

Yield: 8 pint jars

Ingredients:

- Two cups of diced tomatoes
- One cup of chopped bell peppers
- One cup of chopped onions
- One cup of chopped carrots
- Half a cup of chopped celery
- Two cups of cooked black beans
- Two cups of cooked kidney beans
- Two cups of vegetable broth
- Two tablespoons of chili powder
- One tablespoon of ground cumin
- One teaspoon salt
- Half teaspoon black pepper

Directions:

1. In your big pot, mix all fixings, then let it boil on moderate-high temp. Simmer within 15 mins till vegetables are tender.
2. Ladle mixture into your sterilized jars with 1" headspace. Remove any air bubbles using your bubble remover tool.
3. Clean your jar rims, then secure with lids plus bands. Process jars in your pressure canner at 10 PSI within 90 mins.
4. Allow pressure to fully decrease before removing jars from canner. Cool it down within 12-24 hours before checking for proper sealing and storing.

Nutritional Values: Calories 220; Carbs 38g; Fat 1g; Protein 11g

87. Canned Creamed Corn

Preparation time: 30 mins

Cooking time: 15 mins

Processing time: 85 mins

Yield: 8 pint jars

Ingredients:

- Twenty-four cups of fresh corn kernels (about twenty ears of corn)
- One and a half cups of fine granulated sugar
- One-fourth cup of non-iodized salt
- Four cups of water
- Three cups of heavy cream
- Two cups of cold water mixed with two-thirds cup of ClearJel powder

Directions:

1. In your big pot, mix fresh corn kernels, sugar, non-iodized salt, and four cups of water. Let it boil on moderate-high temp. Adjust to a simmer within 10 mins, mixing often.
2. In your big container, mix two-thirds cup ClearJel powder with two cups of cold water. Whisk until no lumps remain.
3. Gradually add the ClearJel mixture into the pot with the cooked corn while stirring continuously.
4. Add heavy cream, then continue to cook within 5 mins till you achieve desired consistency.
5. Fill each sterilized pint jar, leaving one inch of headspace from the rim. Remove any air bubbles using your bubble remover tool.
6. Clean your jar rims, then secure with lids plus bands. Process jars in your pressure canner at 11 PSI (adjusting for altitude) within 85 mins.
7. Allow pressure to fully decrease before removing jars from canner. Cool it down within 12-24 hours before checking for proper sealing and storing.

Nutritional Values: Calories: 349; Carbs: 51g; Fat: 14g; Protein: 7g

88. Classic Canned Beets

Preparation time: 30 mins

Cooking time: 10 mins

Processing time: 30 mins

Yield: 6 pint jars

Ingredients:

- Eight pounds of fresh beets (about twenty-four medium-sized)
- Six cups of water
- Two tablespoons of pickling salt

Directions:

1. Wash and trim the beets, leaving about an inch of stem and root ends.
2. Boil the beets in water within 10 mins till slightly tender. Drain and rinse the beets under cold water. Peel, then cut them into even-sized chunks or slices.
3. Pack the beet chunks tightly into clean jars, leaving one-inch headspace.
4. In your pot, boil six cups of water plus two tablespoons of pickling salt. Pour mixture over beets with 1" headspace. Remove any air bubbles using your bubble remover tool.
5. Clean your jar rims, then secure with lids plus bands. Process jars in your pressure canner at 11 PSI (adjusting for altitude) within 30 mins.
6. Allow pressure to fully decrease before removing jars from canner. Cool it down within 12-24 hours before checking for proper sealing and storing.

Nutritional Values: Calories: 60; Carbs: 14 g; Fat: 0 g; Protein: 2 g

89. Honey-Glazed Carrots

Preparation time: 25 mins

Cooking time: 15 mins

Processing time: 30 mins

Yield: 6 pint jars

Ingredients:

- Eight cups of sliced carrots
- One and a half cups of honey
- Two cups of water
- One tablespoon of lemon juice
- Half a teaspoon of salt

Directions:

1. In your big saucepan, mix honey, water, lemon juice, plus salt. Let it boil, then mix till honey is dissolved. Add sliced carrots to the boiling liquid and cook within 5 mins.
2. Pack carrots tightly into your sterilized jars with 1" headspace. Ladle hot liquid over carrots, maintaining 1" headspace. Remove any air bubbles using your bubble remover tool.
3. Clean your jar rims, then secure with lids plus bands. Process jars in your pressure canner at 10 PSI (adjusting for altitude) within 30 mins.
4. Allow pressure to fully decrease before removing jars from canner. Cool it down within 12-24 hours before checking for proper sealing and storing.

Nutritional Values: Calories: 180; Carbs: 41g; Fat: 0g; Protein: 2g

90. Canned Asparagus Spears

Preparation time: 20 mins

Cooking time: 10 mins

Processing time: 25 mins

Yield: 4 pint jars

Ingredients:

- Four pounds fresh asparagus spears, washed and trimmed
- Four cups water
- One tablespoon coarse sea salt
- Four garlic cloves, peeled and halved

Directions:

1. In your big pot, boil four cups of water. Add asparagus spears, then blanch within 2-3 mins till they turn bright green.
2. Drain the asparagus spears and immediately transfer them to a bowl filled with ice water. Drain.
3. Place two garlic clove halves and 1/4 tablespoon of sea salt into your sterilized jars.
4. Carefully pack cooled asparagus spears into each jar, standing them upright so that they are packed tightly together.
5. Fill each jar with boiling water from your large pot with 1" headspace. Remove any air bubbles using your bubble remover tool.
6. Clean your jar rims, then secure with lids plus bands. Process jars in your pressure canner at 10 PSI (adjusting for altitude) within 25 mins.
7. Allow pressure to fully decrease before removing jars from canner. Cool it down within 12-24 hours before checking for proper sealing and storing.

Nutritional Values: Calories: 30; Carbs: 4.5g; Fat: 0.3g; Protein: 2.5g

91. Spicy Candied Jalapenos

Preparation time: 15 mins

Cooking time: 15 mins

Processing time: 10 mins

Yield: 6 half-pint jars

Ingredients:

- Four cups sliced fresh jalapeno peppers
- Two cups granulated sugar
- One cup apple cider vinegar
- One teaspoon celery seeds
- One teaspoon garlic powder
- Half a teaspoon ground turmeric

Directions:

1. In your big saucepan, mix granulated sugar, apple cider, celery seeds, garlic powder, plus ground turmeric. Let it boil on moderate-high temp, mixing often till sugar dissolves.
2. Add sliced jalapenos, then adjust to moderate-low temp. Cook within 12-14 mins till jalapenos are softened.

3. Pack jalapeno slices into your sterilized jars with ¼" headspace. Add syrup over jalapenos in each jar until just below the rim. Remove any air bubbles using your bubble remover tool.
4. Clean your jar rims, then secure with lids plus bands. Process jars in your pressure canner at 10 PSI (adjusting for altitude) within 10 mins.
5. Allow pressure to fully decrease before removing jars from canner. Cool it down within 12-24 hours before checking for proper sealing and storing.

Nutritional Values: Calories: 98; Carbs: 23g; Fat: 0.5g; Protein: 0.8g

92. Caraway and Ginger Carrots

Preparation time: 20 mins

Cooking time: 10 mins

Processing time: 25 mins

Yield: 6 pint jars

Ingredients:

- Four pounds of carrots, sliced diagonally
- One tablespoon caraway seeds
- Two tablespoons grated fresh ginger
- One and a half teaspoons salt
- Three cups water
- Two cups white vinegar
- One cup granulated sugar

Directions:

1. In your big saucepan, mix water, white vinegar, granulated sugar, caraway seeds, grated ginger, plus salt. Let it boil on moderate-high temp, then cook within 2 mins till sugar dissolves completely.
2. Add sliced carrots, then cook within 5 mins till slightly tender. Remove your saucepan, then carefully fill each prepared jar with the carrot mixture with 1" headspace.
3. Remove any air bubbles using your bubble remover tool.
4. Clean your jar rims, then secure with lids plus bands. Process jars in your pressure canner at 10 PSI (adjusting for altitude) within 25 mins.
5. Allow pressure to fully decrease before removing jars from canner. Cool it down within 12-24 hours before checking for proper sealing and storing.

Nutritional Values: Calories: 110; Carbs: 24g; Fat: 0g; Protein: 2g

93. Cubed White Potatoes

Preparation time: 30 mins

Cooking time: 15 mins

Processing time: 40 mins

Yield: 8 pint jars

Ingredients:

- Eighteen medium white potatoes, peeled & sliced into cubes
- Four cups of water
- Two teaspoons of canning or pickling salt (optional)

Directions:

1. Rinse the cubed potatoes in cold water to remove any remaining dirt or debris.
2. Boil your big pot with water, and lightly blanch cubed potatoes within two mins. Strain, then put aside.
3. If using salt, add 1/4 tsp canning salt to each sterilized jar. Pack the cubed potatoes evenly into your jars with 1" headspace.
4. Pour boiling water over potatoes, maintaining 1" headspace. Remove any air bubbles using your bubble remover tool.
5. Clean your jar rims, then secure with lids plus bands. Process jars in your pressure canner at 11 PSI (adjusting for altitude) within 40 mins.
6. Allow pressure to fully decrease before removing jars from canner. Cool it down within 12-24 hours before checking for proper sealing and storing.

Nutritional Values: Calories: 175; Carbs: 40g; Fat: 0g; Protein: 4g

Chapter 15. MEAT

94. Marinated Beef Hash

Preparation time: 1 hour

Cooking time: 1 hour

Processing time: 1 hour 30 mins

Yield: 6 pint jars

Ingredients:

- Two and a half pounds of lean beef, cubed
- One cup of soy sauce
- One tablespoon of Worcestershire sauce
- Half a teaspoon of ground ginger
- Four tablespoons of olive oil, divided
- Two medium chopped onions
- Four cloves of minced garlic
- Three big peeled & diced russet potatoes
- One & half cups of beef broth

Directions:

1. In your big container, mix cubed beef, soy sauce, Worcestershire, and ground ginger. Cover, then marinate in your refrigerator within 30 mins.
2. In your big skillet, warm up two tablespoons olive oil on moderate temp. Put onions plus garlic, then cook till soft.
3. Take marinated beef, then drain any excess marinade. Add beef to your skillet, then cook till browned.
4. In another big skillet, warm up remaining olive oil on moderate temp. Add diced potatoes, then cook till slightly softened.
5. Combine cooked meat, onions, garlic, potatoes, and beef broth in your big container. Pack hot beef hash mixture into your sterilized jars with 1" headspace.
6. Remove any air bubbles using your bubble remover tool.
7. Clean your jar rims, then secure with lids plus bands. Process jars in your pressure canner at 10 PSI (adjusting for altitude) within 75 mins.
8. Allow pressure to fully decrease before removing jars from canner. Cool it down within 12-24 hours before checking for proper sealing and storing.

Nutritional Values: Calories: 450; Carbs: 46g; Fat: 17g; Protein: 28g

95. Indian Chicken Marsala

Preparation time: 30 mins

Cooking time: 8 mins

Processing time: 75 mins

Yield: 6 servings

Ingredients:

- One & half pounds no bones & skin chicken thighs, sliced into chunks
- One cup chopped yellow onion
- Two cloves garlic (minced)
- One and a half cups sliced cremini mushrooms
- One tablespoon vegetable oil
- One teaspoon cumin, ground
- Half a teaspoon turmeric, ground
- Half a teaspoon garam masala
- Quarter teaspoon red chili powder (adjust according to desired spice level)
- Quarter teaspoon ground coriander
- One fifteen-ounce can diced tomatoes with juice
- Three-quarters cup chicken broth
- Half a cup heavy cream
- Salt & pepper, as required

Directions:

1. In your pressure canner, warm up vegetable oil on moderate temp. Add onion, garlic, plus mushrooms; cook till onions are translucent.
2. Combine the cumin, turmeric, garam masala, red chili powder, and coriander in your small container. Flavor chicken pieces using salt plus pepper.
3. Add seasoned chicken to your pressure canner, mixing well. Add canned tomatoes with juice plus chicken broth; stir well.
4. Close, then lock your pressure canner lid. Set it to high pressure on moderate-high temp, then cook within 8 mins.
5. Release pressure carefully using the quick-release method; carefully remove lid. Check chicken for doneness; return to medium heat if necessary until fully cooked through.
6. Stir in heavy cream; simmer until heated through. Cool it down.
7. Pour cooled Chicken Marsala into your sterilized jars with 1" headspace. Remove any air bubbles using your bubble remover tool.
8. Clean your jar rims, then secure with lids plus bands. Process jars in your pressure canner at 11 PSI (adjusting for altitude) within 75 mins.
9. Allow pressure to fully decrease before removing jars from canner. Cool it down within 12-24 hours before checking for proper sealing and storing.

Nutritional Values: Calories: 300; Carbs: 10g; Fat: 14g; Protein: 30g

96. Beef in Wine Sauce

Preparation time: 30 mins

Cooking time: 1 hour & 15 mins

Processing time: 90 mins

Yield: 6 quarts

Ingredients:

- Two pounds of beef chuck, cubed & pat dried
- One tablespoon salt
- Half a teaspoon black pepper
- One tablespoon of olive oil
- Two cups of red wine, preferably Cabernet Sauvignon or Merlot
- One large onion, chopped
- Three cloves of garlic, minced
- Two cups of beef broth
- Four tablespoons of tomato paste
- One teaspoon of dried rosemary
- One teaspoon of dried thyme
- One bay leaf

Directions:

1. Flavor beef cubes using salt plus black pepper.
2. In your big skillet on moderate temp, then warm up olive oil. Cook beef cubes within 3 to 4 mins per side. Remove beef, then set aside.
3. Deglaze your skillet with red wine. Add onion and garlic, then cook within 5 mins until softened. Pour the onion mixture over the beef in a six-quart pressure canner.
4. Stir in the beef broth, tomato paste, rosemary, thyme, plus bay leaf into your canner. Lock the lid, then set it to high pressure. Cook within 1 hour and 15 mins.
5. After cooking time is done, let the pressure release naturally. Remove the bay leaf from the mixture.
6. Ladle mixture into your sterilized jars with 1" headspace. Remove any air bubbles using your bubble remover tool.
7. Clean your jar rims, then secure with lids plus bands. Process jars in your pressure canner at 10 PSI (adjusting for altitude) within 90 mins.
8. Allow pressure to fully decrease before removing jars from canner. Cool it down within 12-24 hours before checking for proper sealing and storing.

Nutritional Values: Calories: 390; Carbs: 10g; Fat: 20g; Protein: 30g

97. Savory Ground Turkey

Preparation time: 20 mins

Cooking time: 10 mins

Processing time: 90 mins

Yield: 6 pint jars

Ingredients:

- Two pounds ground turkey
- One tablespoon olive oil

- Two teaspoons salt
- One teaspoon pepper
- Two cloves crushed garlic
- One chopped onion
- Half cup diced each red pepper & green pepper
- One cup chopped tomatoes

Directions:

1. Warm up your big skillet on moderate temp. Add olive oil, ground turkey, salt, plus pepper, then cook, stirring occasionally, till turkey is browned.
2. Mix in crushed garlic, chopped onion, diced peppers, plus chopped tomatoes. Continue cooking for an additional 5 mins.
3. Transfer cooked ground turkey mixture into your sterilized jars with 1" headspace. Remove any air bubbles using your bubble remover tool.
4. Clean your jar rims, then secure with lids plus bands. Process jars in your pressure canner at 11 PSI (adjusting for altitude) within 90 mins.
5. Allow pressure to fully decrease before removing jars from canner. Cool it down within 12-24 hours before checking for proper sealing and storing.

Nutritional Values: Calories: 240; Carbs: 7g; Fat: 14g; Protein: 22g

98. Beef with Burgundy

Preparation time: 30 mins

Cooking time: 1 hour

Processing time: 75 mins

Yield: 6 to 7 quarts

Ingredients:

- Three pounds beef, cubed
- One and a half cups all-purpose flour
- One teaspoon ground black pepper
- One tablespoon olive oil
- Half a cup unsalted butter
- Two medium yellow onions, chopped
- Eight cloves of garlic, minced
- Two cups burgundy wine
- Four cups beef broth
- Two tablespoons tomato paste
- Two tablespoons fresh thyme leaves, chopped
- One tablespoon fresh rosemary leaves, chopped
- Four bay leaves

- Four cups fresh mushrooms, sliced

Directions:

1. Mix flour plus ground pepper in your big container. Add beef cubes, then coat them evenly with the flour mixture.
2. In your big skillet, warm up olive oil plus butter on moderate-high temp. Brown the beef till well-browned on all sides.
3. Place the browned beef in a pressure canner along with their drippings.
4. In your same skillet, cook onions plus garlic till softened and fragrant. Add them to the pressure canner.
5. Pour burgundy wine into your skillet to deglaze it. Let it simmer briefly mins before pouring it to your pressure canner.
6. Stir in beef broth, tomato paste, thyme, rosemary, and bay leaves into the pressure canner. Close and lock the lid, then process at 10-pounds pressure within 60 mins.
7. Once done, release pressure following manufacturer's instructions; remove lid away from you so you won't be harmed by releasing steam. Check the consistency of the sauce. If necessary, simmer briefly to thicken.
8. Sautee mushrooms in a separate pan with some butter until cooked and stir them into the beef mixture just before canning.
9. Ladle hot beef and burgundy mixture into your sterilized quart jars with 1" headspace. Clean your jar rims, then secure with lids plus bands. Process jars in your pressure canner at 10 PSI (adjusting for altitude) within 75 mins.
10. Allow pressure to fully decrease before removing jars from canner. Cool it down within 12-24 hours before checking for proper sealing and storing.

Nutritional Values: Calories: 540; Carbs: 34g; Fat: 22g; Protein: 39g

99. Italian Chicken Cacciatore

Preparation time: 30 mins

Cooking time: 15 mins

Processing time: 75 mins

Yield: 6 pint jars

Ingredients:

- Two and a half pounds of chicken parts, skin removed
- One cup of all-purpose flour

- One teaspoon sea salt
- Half teaspoon black pepper
- Quarter cup of olive oil
- Four cloves garlic, minced
- One large onion, chopped
- One and a half cups red bell peppers, chopped
- One and a half cups green bell peppers, chopped
- Four cups canned crushed tomatoes
- Two cups sliced mushrooms
- One cup red wine (optional)
- Two teaspoons dried oregano
- Two teaspoons dried basil

Directions:

1. In your shallow container, mix flour, salt, plus pepper. Warm up olive oil in your big skillet on moderate-high temp.
2. Dredge chicken in flour mixture, then carefully place it in the hot oil. Cook till browned on all sides.
3. Remove chicken, then set aside on paper towels to drain any excess oil.
4. In your same skillet, sauté garlic, onion, plus bell peppers till slightly softened. Add crushed tomatoes, mushrooms, red wine (if using), oregano, and basil to the skillet. Let it simmer.
5. Add browned chicken pieces, then cook within 10 mins till chicken is cooked through. Ladle hot Chicken Cacciatore into your sterilized jars with 1" headspace.
6. Clean your jar rims, then secure with lids plus bands. Process jars in your pressure canner at 10 PSI (adjusting for altitude) within 75 mins.
7. Allow pressure to fully decrease before removing jars from canner. Cool it down within 12-24 hours before checking for proper sealing and storing.

Nutritional Values: Calories: 410; Carbs: 29g; Fat: 18g; Protein: 30g

100.   Simple Beef Stew

Preparation time: 20 minutes

Cooking time: 90 minutes

Processing time: 75 minutes

Yield: 6 servings

Ingredients:

- One pound of beef, cubed
- Two medium-sized potatoes, diced
- One large onion, chopped
- One cup of carrots, sliced
- Three cups of beef broth

- Half cup of celery, sliced
- Half cup of green peas
- One tablespoon of all-purpose flour
- One teaspoon of salt
- Half teaspoon of black pepper
- Two tablespoons of vegetable oil

Directions:

1. Warm up vegetable oil in your pressure cooker on moderate temp. Add cubed beef, then cook till browned. Add chopped onion, then cook till softened.
2. Sprinkle all-purpose flour, then mix till coated. Mix in diced potatoes, sliced carrots, celery, green peas, salt, black pepper, plus beef.
3. Close your pressure cooker lid, then set it to high pressure on high temp. Cook within 45 mins. Carefully release pressure naturally.
4. Fill your sterilized jars with hot beef stew mixture with 1" headspace.
5. Clean your jar rims, then secure with lids plus bands. Process jars in your pressure canner at 11 PSI (adjusting for altitude) within 75 mins.
6. Allow pressure to fully decrease before removing jars from canner. Cool it down within 12-24 hours before checking for proper sealing and storing.

Nutritional Values: Calories: 325; Carbs: 34g; Fat: 11g; Protein: 20g

Bonus 1: Foods You Can Prepare Without Appliance

If you are a harried parent, a busy young professional, a bachelor, or don't really love cooking, the "no-cook" meals are ideal for your lifestyle. Besides, at times when you don't have access to a stove – say while camping or during a kitchen renovation, a no-cook meal can be an exceptional option.

Saving time and money in the kitchen by not using any appliances is a terrific idea. Not only that, but you can also make healthy meals without any fuss. The purpose of this chapter is to show you how to cook meals without using any appliances. This can be a lifesaver if you're short on time or have limited kitchen space. There are many options for no-cook meals that are both healthy and delicious. Some of the best no-cook meals include:

1. Salads: Salads are a great way to get your entire days' worth of nutrients in one sitting. They're also fantastic for recycling scraps of dinner. There are a lot of different salad recipes out there, so you're sure to find one that you love. Some of our favorites include tuna salad, chickpea salad, and Greek salad.

2. Wraps: Wraps are another great way to pack a lot of food into a small amount of time. They are also an excellent method for recycling previously prepared foods. You can make wraps from anything, and they're perfect for lunch or dinner. Some of our favorite wraps include the buffalo chicken wrap, the salmon wrap, and the turkey wrap.

3. Burritos: Burritos are another great option for a no-cook meal. They're quick and easy to make, and they're perfect for a quick lunch or dinner. You can make them with anything you have on hand, and they're always a hit. Some of the favorite burrito recipes include the chicken burrito, the beef burrito, and the vegetarian burrito.

4. Tacos: Tacos are also a great way to pack a healthy meal to go. Whether you're making them for a street fair, catering an event, or just grabbing a quick lunch on the go, tacos are a great choice. Some common taco recipes include the chicken taco, the shrimp taco, the fish taco, the ground turkey taco, and others.

5. Soups: Soups are another classic no-cook meal. You can make a delicious gazpacho, a delicious minestrone soup, a delicious cream of mushroom soup, a delicious cream of tomato soup, a delicious tomato soup, and more.

6. Sandwiches: Sandwiches are a great way to eat a healthy sandwich on the go. You can add lettuce, tomato, cheese, or anything else on hand that you'd like to add to your sandwich.

Cooking without appliances can be a time-saving and money-saving way to make healthy meals. Salads, wraps, burritos, tacos, and soups are all great options, and there are many different recipes to choose from. But feel free to experiment and find your own favorite combination that you like.

Bonus 2: Foods you can prepare while away from home

In an ideal world, you would be able to prepare all of your meals at home and eat them whenever you wanted, but that's not the situation in today's modern society. Most people eat their meals in a variety of locations, including their homes, workplaces, and even cars. There are numerous restaurants and takeout options available, but sadly, the majority of these selections don't adhere to a healthy eating plan. As a result, planning healthy meals in advance is crucial to keeping up a healthy lifestyle.

The best way to make sure you're getting a healthy meal is to make it yourself. This doesn't mean you have to cook a complicated dish—you can easily pack a sandwich or a salad and eat it on the go. Or, if you're traveling, you can typically pack more than enough food to last you throughout your trip. It just takes a little forethought.

For reference, here are some foods you can prep ahead of time:

1. Make sure you pack plenty of healthy snacks to keep you going during your trip. This will help you avoid eating out and save you money. Some good options include trail mix, fruits, and granola.
2. It's also a good idea to pack plenty of water to stay hydrated. Stay away from sugary drinks and limit your intake of foods containing artificial sweeteners.
3. Make sure to pack a healthy breakfast. This will help you start your day off on the right foot and give you the energy you need to get through your day. Some good options include oatmeal, yogurt, and fruit.
4. Finally, make sure to pack a healthy lunch. This will help you take the break you need and avoid feeling ravenous later in the day. This doesn't mean you have to pack a heavy meal— simply pack a light meal that will tide you over until dinner. Some good options include sandwiches, salads, and fruit.

If you're looking to eat healthy while away from home, packing a few dishes is a great way to go. You can easily prepare sandwiches, salads, and even breakfast foods like oatmeal and yogurt. But if you're going to be gone for a while, you should probably bring more than just a few simple dishes. By packing a few healthy snacks and drinks, as well as enough food for lunch and dinner, you'll be able to stick to your healthy eating plan without having to worry about finding food on the go.

Conclusion

Thank you for making it through this cookbook! Canning preserves food by slowing down the spoilage caused by microorganisms such as yeasts and molds. These microorganisms grow naturally on all foods. Canning at high temperatures kills these microbes, making it possible to store food for long periods of time without refrigeration.

Canning methods cover a wide range. The main reason why you should start water bath canning is the health benefits. Preserving foods can make them last a lot longer, but it can also help you protect the vitamins and nutrients that are often diminished with other preservation methods. Water bath canning is the best way to preserve those foods you love to eat all year round, and it's easy to do when you have the right equipment.

You'll preserve the most nutrients when using a water bath canner to put up your vegetables and home-canned fruit. The canning process makes the food last much longer. Many people prefer using this method because it doesn't add chemicals as other forms do, so the food doesn't lose its flavor over time.

Water bath canning is one of the best ways to preserve food, but it can be a little bit tricky at first. It's essential to keep things clean and organized throughout the entire process so that you don't end up putting your family in danger.

So, that's it! We hope you've found this water bath canning and preserving cookbook helpful. We recommend using it to preserve your favorite vegetables and fruits all year round. You can also use it to preserve meats, and as a great way to make sure there's never a waste of food!

Made in United States
Orlando, FL
31 August 2024

51001099R00059